M000101360

Power Branding Secrets

Power Branding Secrets

SPARK CUSTOMER INTEREST
AND IGNITE YOUR SALES

❖ ❖ ❖

Edwin Dearborn

Copyright © 2015 Edwin Dearborn
All rights reserved.

ISBN: 0996313206
ISBN 13: 9780996313209
Library of Congress Control Number: 2015906465
Dearborn Media Group, Irvin, CA

Dedication

I dedicate this book to the person who always believed in me and saw nothing but goodness in my heart, my mother Jackie. To those who do not believe that angels exist among us on Earth have evidently never met my mother. And to my father Ed, thank you for your courage as a Marine, the moments we played football together and the many fishing trips across this great nation.

Acknowledgements

WHILE PERSISTENCE ON MY PART was crucial to complete and publish this book, the work would never have been possible without the efforts, support, belief and patience of many people within my life.

To my wife Carlie, and my four children Alexandra, Makenna, Lily Rae and Rohan, you have all put up with my neglect of your needs for mine, so that I was able to accomplish many endeavors in my life. Each of you is my best friend and together you are my most important legacy.

To my parents Ed and Jackie, my life is filled with endearing memories because of your hard work, support and boundless love. To my brother Mike, stay crazy, outrageous and outspoken.

To the generations of Forefathers before me, thank you for believing in and fighting for the greatest nation to grace the Earth. To our troops, past, present and future... I am eternally indebted to your service and sacrifice.

To my best friend Matt Judkin, keep the flame of freedom alive in your heart; may your future days be filled with purpose and long motorcycle rides. To my buddies Cindi & Eron Boyer, love you both forever. To all the dedicated members of my church, you are always in my heart, and our work together remains among my best memories and accomplishments. To my fellow misfits and rebel souls at The Lost Bean in Tustin, CA - keep the coffee hot and organic.

To all my fellow motorcycle riders that I've never met personally, but who waved hello or signaled a sign of brotherhood to me as we passed each other on innumerable highways across this fine land, keep the rubber side down and stay rebellious always.

To the authors that inspired me to write this book, Grant Cardone, David Meerman Scott, Dorie Clark, David Jenyns, Craig Brockie and Bill McIntosh, thank you for your words and enthusiasm for your underappreciated craft. To Robert Stover, my book would not have achieved the level of quality it has without your insight and coaching, and I am deeply indebted to you for that. To my editor and fellow author, Ronald Joseph Kule (RonKuleBooks.com), thanks for your support, experience, late nights and insight. To Marty Gottlieb, thanks so much for your creativity for the design of my book cover.

And to L. Ron Hubbard, the author that redefined the respected title. More people on this fine Earth will soon discover your genius, wise words and humanity, and will become better people for it.

Just like I have.

Preface

HOW DOES ONE CREATE AND mold a powerful brand? How do we then catapult it upon the world? The answer: with brilliant marketing, genuine care, sharp content and a deft use of social media and PR.

More importantly, how do we position ourselves as leaders, clear experts within our given arena, and create a voluminous amount of bonafide leads and revenue?

When all is said and done, we want more people to perceive our brand as a *Power Brand*. I define *Power Brand* as the one that is perceived to be the most positive choice for our recipients - one that resonates at such a genuine and emotional level that consumers know with unshakable certainty that our brand is the one to purchase. And to share with others. A *Power Brand* allures inquisitive minds into our messages, compelling the "I want that" in their minds, thus converting them into new and brand-loyal customers.

I wrote *Power Branding Secrets* to help small businesses, entrepreneurs and startups to develop brands that grow into enduring, profitable enterprises. My purpose is to revive the ultimate *Power Brand* - America - and thus her economy. A small band of tireless entrepreneurs, energetic innovators, and emphatic voices can reignite the American small business culture by retooling their branding and business protocols and filling in the gaps of omitted know-how.

Building a *Power Brand* requires proven and tested know-how, hard work, ingenuity, creativity, humility and a tremendous amount of bull-headed determination. Power brands are meticulously and systematically built. The elements of a *Power Brand* form into a previously unidentified triangle, described and discussed in detail within this book. Brand-image development is a long-term process, but one well worth the work, as it is an effective weapon in earning prospective customers' attention, interest, and brand loyalty.

People within our society are quite conscious and concerned about their personal status and how they are perceived by others. They prefer to purchase branded products and services that showcase their status and position in life to their friends and to the world at large. Customers rely on branded products and services in order to be recognized and respected, as well as to reassure their own self-worth. They prefer to purchase from established brands, even when the price for doing so costs more than a non-branded product or service.

A Power Brand is a highly effective power play that catapults brand awareness above that of competitors, thus creating a definitive edge for your marketing, business development, and revenue.

A *Power Brand* owns a distinct piece of geography within their customer's mind map.

Moreover, a *Power Brand* permits customers to see a product or service as something more than utilitarian. Your brand becomes a part of something significant in their lives and is interwoven into their feeling of security and sense of well-being, providing a richer existence. *Power Branding* achieves previously unrealized benefits for your business or startup and it achieves these by telling people four important components of your story:

1. Who you are.
2. What you do.
3. How you do it.
4. Why you do it.

When a brand clearly and consistently answers these questions, from their identity, their customer services and how they stay connected with their audience with branded content, they can thrive in any economy. And they are a *Power Brand.*

CHAPTER 1

America The Brand: How to Revive Her

"AMERICA" IS A *POWER BRAND.* In fact, America is the ultimate power brand. A look through history reveals the impact that America has had upon the world as well as other power brands that have emanated from this country. When you list out the leaders, philosophers, artists, musicians, actors, scientists, inventors and world-renowned businesses that America has produced, you end up with voluminous pages of *Power Brands.* Some of America's *Power Brands* are recognized and cherished around the globe: Disneyland and Hollywood; the Los Angeles Lakers and the New York Yankees; Google and Facebook; Apple and Microsoft; Michael Jordan and Elvis Presley, to name a few. America is the largest, most successful incubator of some of the planet's most iconic and influential *Power Brands.*

AMERICA IS NOT ONLY THE WORLD'S No. 1 *POWER BRAND,* BUT IS THE WORLD'S BIGGEST INCUBATOR OF POWER BRANDS!

The *Power Brand* that is America was conceived of and forged by true entrepreneurs and innovators. Our American Forefathers would not accept taxation without their representation. Together, they formed their own currency and mission statement, declaring their independence from the oppressive economic model that was suppressing their entrepreneurial aspirations and families' well-being. More than for any other reason, these patriots decided to revolt and wage war over the issue of economic freedom.

Therefore, we are a nation founded upon the spirit of entrepreneurial rebellion, spurred on and inspired not only to achieve greatness, but also to secure equal pursuits of happiness.

THE CROWN WAS JEALOUS OF OUR EMERGING *POWER BRAND*

During the mid-1700's, Britain was at its height of power but she was also heavily in debt. Since the creation of the Bank of England, the British had suffered four costly wars. The total debt stood at £140,000,000 – in those days a boatload of money.

In order to make interest payments to the bank, the British government legislated a program to raise revenues from their American colonies, largely through an extensive program of taxation.

A shortage of material prevented the minting of coins in the colonies, so in 1764, the Colonials began to print their own paper money, which they called Colonial Scrip. This was very successful as a means of exchange and gave the colonies a sense of identity. Colonial Scrip was debt-free paper money not backed by gold or silver. It was so successful that the British Crown created counterfeit colonial scrip in an effort to devalue Colonial Scrip and create a distrust with its usage.

While he visited Britain, The Bank of England asked Benjamin Franklin how he would account for the new-found prosperity in the colonies. Franklin replied, "That is simple. In the colonies we issue our own money. It is called Colonial Scrip. We issue it in proper proportion to the demands of trade and industry to make the products pass easily from the producers to the consumers. In this manner, creating for ourselves our own paper money, we control its purchasing power and we have no interest to pay to no one."

Colonial American leaders had learned that The People's confidence in the currency was all they needed, and that they could be free of incurring debt, free of the Bank of England.

In response, the world's most powerful independent bank at the time used its influence over the British parliament to press for the passing of the Currency Act of 1764, making it illegal for the colonies to print their own money and forcing them to pay all future taxes to Britain in silver or gold.

Here is what Franklin said after that: "In one year, the conditions were so reversed that the era of prosperity ended, and a depression set in to such an extent that the streets of the Colonies were filled with unemployed."

Franklin also noted in his autobiography, "The colonies would gladly have borne the little tax on tea and other matters had it not been that England took away from the colonies their money, which created unemployment and dissatisfaction. The inability of the colonists to get power to issue their own money permanently, and out of the hands of George III and the international bankers, was the PRIME reason for the Revolutionary War."

THE VITAL ROLE OF THE AMERICAN SMALL BUSINESS

Small business is the backbone and cornerstone of the American economy today. In fact, second only to our veterans and men and women in uniform, American entrepreneurs and small business owners are our greatest heroes because they create jobs for Americans and they inspire real hope that in America anyone can rule their own destiny – a hope for financial independence.

I firmly believe that success is the small business owner's patriotic duty. When he succeeds, he creates greater employment opportunities for other Americans, which instigates economic growth for our nation. Strong, small businesses build a powerful, more prosperous America.

Over two-hundred and thirty years later, America is an economic superpower still driven by entrepreneurs, innovators and small business owners. Here are some interesting statistics from the Small Business Administration (2012) of how small businesses shape and drive our economy:

* 64 percent of net, new private-sector jobs
* 49.2 percent of private-sector employment
* 42.9 percent of private-sector payroll
* 46 percent of private-sector output
* 43 percent of high-tech employment
* 33 percent of exporting value

Want to see the unemployment numbers drop? Help the small business owner. Want to see growth in our Gross Domestic Product (GDP)? Help the small business owner. I believe that America is only one generation away from an unprecedented economic renaissance, if we greatly assist the small business owner to succeed.

Seeing this same vision, crowdfunding companies such as Crown Funding Planning in Santa Ana, California, are providing needed mentorship, training programs and direction for small businesses and startups, even non-profits, so they can intelligently and correctly generate needed investment funding while not incurring debt. There is no doubt that this rapidly emerging industry will continue to grow into a massive resource for many American small businesses and startups. I see its future: crowdfunding will become even more popular and comprehensive with time.

Coming together as dedicated entrepreneurs and mentors, helping small businesses grow into ***Power Brands***, we will only strengthen and further secure the ultimate ***Power Brand***, America.

And so we work.

CHAPTER 2

The Current State of Small
Business in America

HOW SMALL BUSINESSES HAVE FARED since the economic recession of 2008 is a barometer of the American economy as a whole.

"Small businesses are core to America's economic competitiveness. Not only do they employ half of the nation's private sector workforce – about 120 million people – but since 1995 they have created approximately two-thirds of the net new jobs in our country. Yet in recent years, small businesses have been slow to recover from a recession and credit crisis that hit them especially hard.

"Small businesses are critical to job creation in the U.S. economy. Small businesses create two out of every three net new jobs. Small firms employ half of the private sector workforce, and since 1995 small businesses have created about two out of every three net new jobs—65 percent of total net job creation.

"Small businesses were hit harder than larger businesses during the 2008 financial crisis, and have been slower to recover from a recession of unusual depth and duration. Small firms were hit harder than large firms during the crisis, with the smallest firms hit hardest. Between 2007 and 2012, the small business share of total net job losses was about 60 percent." - Harvard Business School (July 22, 2014)

To add fuel to the fire, small business people are finding it almost impossible to be able to qualify for loans, since the majority of prospective borrowers suffer from credit problems induced during the recession. Economic growth that was the intended result of massive stimulant packages were killed by banks when their lending restrictions became too restrictive to the average American wanting to start a new business.

Experts in Academia and in business agree that small businesses must be able to access capital and credit, if they are to begin their journey to success. Unlike big corporations, small businesses do not have the same access to equity capital markets. And banks simply find it not profitable to loan money to small businesses any longer.

"Transaction costs to process a $100,000 loan are comparable to a $1 million loan, but with less profit. As a result, banks are less likely to engage in lending at the smallest dollar level. Some banks, particularly larger banks, have significantly reduced or eliminated loans below a certain threshold, typically $100,000 or $250,000, or simply will not lend to small businesses with revenue of less than $2 million, as a way to limit time-consuming applications from small businesses. This is problematic as over half of small businesses surveyed are seeking loans of under $100,000, leaving a critical gap in the small business loan market." - Harvard Business School (July 22, 2014)

As mentioned earlier, the massive growth of crowdfunding has led to the popularity of funding resources such as KickStarter and Indiegogo, reviving hope and access to capital for many small businesses and startups. However, these entities are not the new "magic bullet" for anyone needing capital for a good idea. Instead, branding and organizational acumen and processes remain what is required to convince investors, small and large, to invest.

THE ENEMIES OF AMERICAN SMALL BUSINESS

The American small business person's enemies consist of ever-increasing layers of new technology, growth challenges, and communication barriers. Economic freedom is best achieved today not through armed insurrection, but through better know-how, branding and marketing prowess, organizational efficiency, improved training, and the generation of viable sales levels. Imagine what courage it takes today to start and manage a successful business among these daunting factors:

- Taxes that keep rising.
- Federal and municipal government regulations that are becoming more onerous and numerous.
- A litigious environment where you can be sued over almost anything.
- Stiffer global competition.
- Economic uncertainty – the highest since the Great Depression.
- A widening gap of wealth, as the middle class is squeezed.
- Increasing minimum-wage requirements.
- Business owners propagandized as greedy and selfish.
- Technology advances moving at breakneck speeds.
- Tighter access to credit from banks, making it all but impossible to borrow funds.
- The cost of continuing education inflating faster than any other market.

Despite these very real dangers and challenges, one I have not mentioned is the most dangerous enemy of all.

THE ULTIMATE ENEMY OF TODAY'S BUSINESS PROFESSIONAL

When one attempts to start a business, he will be approached and pitched by charlatans selling "voodoo" (empty promises). Some of this voodoo is quite expensive; all of it is, unfortunately, extremely ineffective. In the fields of branding and marketing many would-be "experts" exist. (In the latter part of this book, I list the people that I look up to and see as legitimate experts within the fields of business, branding, marketing and sales. Understandably, these true professionals tend to be expensive. They will not get hired by 98 percent of small business persons and startups operating on shoestring budgets.)

For businesses on a small budget, time management becomes more important and a vital, premium commodity. One has to find quick solutions for everyday business needs and for marketing and branding challenges; hence, this book's information is timely.

THE BIGGEST ENEMY IS A CRITICAL GAP IN PRAGMATIC KNOW-HOW

Reader, this gap is not your fault. You are putting practically everything on the line to get by and to make your business or startup dreams become a reality and a success. There are only so many days in a week, hours in a day and minutes in an hour.

To solve branding and business problems, you have three available options:

1. Keep doing what you have been doing, coping as best you can.
2. Hire outside professionals and organizations to address your needs.
3. Build up your business with good personnel, know-how and organizational skills.

Option No. 1 is what too many business professionals call "routine," the "daily grind," or state, "It is what it is." This is a sure-fire route to burn-out, heart attack, stress and bankruptcy. Some owners cave in and succumb rapidly; others take as long as 30 years to burn out.

Option No. 2 is an effective means to grow your business, as long as you work with competent individuals and companies that deliver at least what they promise. Legitimate offers to coach, consult and advise have value and can ease your time crunches, bringing about greater productivity and profitability. I like to consider myself and my services within this category.

You will find, though, that many people who talk a big game cannot deliver the goods. They can be quite convincing, but nothing comes about from the relationship in terms of more efficiency, bigger profits or real results. As a small-business owner you need results... *and fast!*

Option No. 3 is the path towards long-term growth, stability, higher profits and satisfaction. This option requires you and your team members to become better educated and proficient at building and managing a business. ***Power Branding Secrets*** fits within this scheme.

Power Branding Secrets is a compendium and a workbook meant to be read and applied. New ideas and innovations to build *your **Power Brand*** will come from specific tips and tools contained herein, with which you can build brand-management strategies that you can implement and track, from which you can expect results.

The ultimate branding and marketing expert for your ***Power Brand*** must become YOU. By filling in your critical gap of pragmatic know-how, you can become the driver of your own V-12 ***Power Brand***.

CHAPTER 3

My Personal Pursuit of the American Dream

I GREW UP THE OLDEST son of small business owners. I worked at my parent's small business during my summers in the 1970's and 80's. Not matters of choice, my jobs were about economic survival for our family. When my teen-aged contemporaries hit the sand and surf at Newport Beach, California, or vacationed in far-away lands, I cleaned motorhomes at 13 years of age, because my parents owned A&D Motorhomes in Costa Mesa, California. Later, when we moved to Irvine, California, I worked there.

Branding and marketing were first introduced to me when I was 19 years old. In 1983, my parents had started another small business, a travel agency, in Irvine. Our marketing efforts consisted of handing out simple fliers that I had produced with rub-on letters and a small copier located in the back of the office. I created a new flier every week and handed out hundreds of these to small- and medium-sized businesses situated in surrounding business parks. With these flyers and the small Sunday advertisements that we ran in our local paper, we generated over a million dollars in sales within our first year of business. In 1984, a million dollars in sales was pretty impressive for a family-owned business and to an impressionable teenager.

I now possessed first-hand knowledge that effective marketing was a crucial factor for business success.

A few years later, I worked for a boutique advertising agency, J. Brooks Potter, in Orange County, California. This exciting career change presented to me an opportunity to meet hundreds of small-and-medium-sized-business professionals, who struggled with branding and how to take their wares and messages to the marketplace. At this time, I read books by David Ogilvy and Jack Trout & Al Ries, renowned leaders in the fields of marketing and branding. (Their books are classics that I still reference 30 years later.)

Working diligently at the agency for over a year, involved in solving many marketing challenges, I observed two important factors: the struggles and confusions of entrepreneurs and business owners with passion, often wavering in their determination to succeed, implementing new strategies and tactics that would brand and market their businesses successfully. On the other side of that coin were marketing professionals working to develop their clients' challenges into new brands and marketing messages by crafting intelligent, innovative programs and stunning marketing materials.

The constant juxtaposition of these two worlds of business owners and advertising professionals, gave me a unique perspective that created a lasting impression on me and the way I envision effective branding in today's business world.

I learned that between the struggle and the creativity a solution can always be discovered, which can be carefully engineered and deployed. When ambitious people in business connect with creatively competent branding professionals, businesses develop and grow into significant entities. I have seen this first-hand so many times that I now find it comical when approached by people attempting to sell me excuses for why someone cannot succeed in business.

During my tenure at that dynamic advertising agency, I was introduced to a young and ambitious doctor, Dr. William Gillette. We met one day at my church and, after speaking with him for some hours, the good doctor believed that we should rebrand his practice and expand it to new heights. He offered me a compensation package that was too good to turn down. I became the marketing director of his wellness practice located in Whittier, California, and in less than a year we increased his practice's revenue by 350 percent.

Did we change his services? No. Did we improve the quality of his services? Not really. We opted to rebrand his practice. And then we aggressively marketed his services... and grew beyond our wildest dreams. In less than two years, he was able to purchase a second practice in Huntington Beach, California. At the tender age of 24, I had propelled the good doctor into millionaire status.

TODAY'S WORLD OF MARKETING HAS CHANGED

In 2007, I knew the world of marketing was transforming radically and rapidly. It was moving faster, and I was not keeping pace with technology. Even the word "blog" seemed ominous and beyond my skill set at the time. The handwriting was on the wall for me: like an old bull I was on the path to pasture if I did not retool my know-how and sharpen my ability to apply what I could learn. If I did not change, I would end up immortalized in some historical museum right next to the Edsel and the Dodo Bird.

Frankly, actually, this new, emerging world of online marketing scared the living crap out of me!

But, I knew that my future survival in business depended on evolving and increasing my know-how.

I sublimated my fears and turned them into an earnest desire for more information. I wanted to learn and to adapt. Knowing that I had to re-engineer my knowledge base and abilities for this "Brave New (2.0) World," I turned to a trusted friend, Bill McIntosh. Bill had created for himself quite some fame on YouTube and he was making a killing with his online businesses. I worked with him, learned a lot, and then started to blog on my own.

Looking back at my original blog posts, the quality of my work was... well, I cringe with embarrassment. At the time that I wrote them, though, I felt alive: now a part of this new, fast-paced, online world that, at first, had awed and baffled me. Now, though, I was a for-real, semi-professional "blogger!"

TECHNICAL UPGRADE

Shortly after, my technical-upgrade journey continued with *The New Rules of Marketing & PR,* by David Meerman Scott. The book became my new marketing scripture – one that I still to this day recommend avidly to anyone I come across. When I first picked it up, I read it daily, testing Scott's words, learning to confront a plethora of new terms and new technology. I was overwhelmed, but equally excited and intrigued by how much the world of branding and marketing had changed. I saw the worlds of the humanities and business connecting, sharing content, and trading ideas like never before. The global scene and its playwrights had changed, and I knew that I had to take a vibrant role in that play's script!

Besides Scott's book, I followed leading bloggers, who covered a wide array of new topics. As a result, I defined and sorted out a rather large body of terminology in the new world of online-marketing technology.

MOTIVATION

I was hooked and I never looked back. Filled with enthusiasm and success, my experiences, studies and interactions with thousands of entrepreneurs and business owners from all types of industries led me to write this book to share my success and what data I gained.

But, let's be honest here, you're reading this book because you wish to perfect your livelihood and to generate greater prosperity for not only for yourself and your family, but also for the future generations of America, right?

It's true what experts say: when conducted correctly, branding and marketing have a positive impact on your life and everyone else's prosperity. You see, I know that most individuals do not desire prosperity because of a financial greed. Most business-minded people and hard-working entrepreneurs are driven by a higher purpose — a sublime, internal fire. This may be their motivation to feed a family, send a son or a daughter to college, pay for a retirement cabin in Angel Fire, New Mexico where the grandchildren on warm summer days fish for hours... or to improve their community, their nation, and the world.

The desire to take an integral role in this wild, chaotic, global game of digital media, of which we are all, to some degree, inextricably a part, is arousing stuff for you and me.

My purpose with ***Power Branding Secrets*** is simple and direct: to open a door to wisdom for those who wish to become wildly successful in for-profit or non-profit enterprises. I want to assist your understanding of these vibrant and fascinating subjects of branding and content marketing. In turn, I wish you to help me revive the greatest *Power Brand* and search engine the world has ever known: America and the American economy.

CHAPTER 4

W.W.W. ~ (The) World Wants Wisdom

(AUTHOR'S NOTE: A STABLE DATUM on which my book is based is that the resolution of any confusion in a field of study begins with a comprehensive knowledge of the basic terminology of the subject.)

In big cities and small villages, people around the world delve deeply into the Internet primarily to do one thing: SEARCH. Google, Bing, Yahoo, YouTube and all of our social-media channels are "Search Engines." I find it amazing that somehow we have all agreed, wittingly or unwittingly, that *"Search"* is the best term to place in front of the word, *Engine*.

I simply cannot imagine it being referred to any other way than *Search Engine*.

Some of us search for directions to our local bank or the nearest dry cleaners. Many of us search for connections with deeper, richer understandings of the world around us. The way I see it, the World Wide Web (www.) really means the *World Wants Wisdom*.

Aren't we all searching for Wisdom… for those things that we can learn so that we can be happier or which can improve our lives? Is that not why we search for Wisdom? Inherently, I think, we want to understand ourselves and our world with greater clarity.

We are, at heart, wisdom seekers.

My hope is that someone, someday, will conceive and launch a search engine named "Socrates." Socrates will index and rank websites, content and forums based on their pragmatic levels of wisdom. No ads, no paid methods pushing up unwise content. Socrates' tag line could be, *"Find True Wisdom."* Imagine how popular that search engine would be!

TERMINOLOGY DEFINED

As promised earlier, to begin in earnest we simply must examine the key definitions of what I feel are the most important terms at this time, which will "decode" and define the fields of branding and content marketing. In future editions, these terms will most likely have to change, or have more words added. In 10 years, there may be hundreds more of basic words that need to be defined and understood. Future critics and marketing pundits may contend that I omitted some crucial terms here. So be it; I did not write this book for them. I wrote for the ambitious student, the willing entrepreneur, and the intrepid small business owners of now and of the future.

SOCRATES: WHERE WISDOM BEGINS

Words and symbols are fundamental to many forms of communication. Whether expressed verbally, in writing, on video, or within music, words and symbols help us communicate with others so as to be understood.

Books and courses are composed of paragraphs, sentences and ultimately into individual words. Words have exact meanings in the contexts in which they are used. When we do not understand the meaning of a word in the context in which it is being used, we struggle in study and become frustrated.

Greek Philosopher Socrates rightfully stated it many years ago, "The beginning of wisdom is the definition of terms."

Opening the door to new wisdom and its application to our lives mandates that we work hard to possess a deep and personal understanding of its basic terminology. To understand branding and content marketing, or any subject we care to learn, we must fully grasp and be able to converse with the nomenclature.

Branding and content marketing, like any other intricate subject, index hundreds of important terms used by their practitioners on a daily basis. To the newbie these sound like Latin or Greek. To realize the full benefits of branding and marketing, defining and understanding their basic words alone will establish a firm-enough foundation on which to springboard forward progress.

I know with total certainty, based on my personal experiences and the results that I have been able to achieve with other businesses, that branding and marketing will most definitely help anyone attain their business and financial goals, when understood and conducted systematically.

I also believe that, correctly applied, branding and marketing can convey and demonstrate wisdom to anyone anywhere in the world. It can help people find pragmatic answers to whatever they seek, including real meaning for their lives.

Voltaire: "Define Your Terms"

To Voltaire, a defining of terms was necessary to any discussion. The 18th century French writer, historian and philosopher wrote, "If you wish to converse with me, define your terms."

Voltaire offered a modernistic approach to understanding compared to the rigorous reasoning of Socrates; namely, *the power and value of careful, empirical science.*

In my opinion, I believe that branding and marketing should be held to the same standard, empirical process as any science. How can one fight the enemies of new ideas and overcome the superstition of old ones, if one cannot establish a science based on a fundamental set of clearly defined terms?

To Voltaire, science and the discussion of the many factors of his (and our) world, could not occur if terms describing objects, phenomenon and other occurrences could not be clearly defined. To be able to apply science to branding and marketing requires the study and understanding of the definitions of their basic terms.

Certainty and Competency

The book *The Way to Happiness*, (www.thewaytohappiness.org) also highlights the importance of defining terms, and how this results in greater competence:

"There are ways to study so that one really learns and can use what one learns. In brief, it consists of having a teacher and/or texts that know what they are talking about; of clearing up every word one does not fully understand; of consulting other references and/or the scene of the subject; sorting out the false data one might already have: sifting the false from the true on the basis of what is now true for you. The end result will be certainty and potential competence." - The Way to Happiness, Chapter 17, "Be Competent."

Through the ages of Mankind, the greatest minds have remarked upon the important and symbiotic relationship among terminology, ability, understanding, and discourse. And in the course of these pages we do not stray from that line of wisdom.

Minimum understanding leads to minimum execution. We, therefore, deduce that a greater understanding of important terms will lead us to greater execution and bettered results.

CHAPTER 5
What is Branding?

WITHOUT BRANDING, YOU ARE A regular person or an average company. Honestly, regular people and average companies do not attract too much attention, nor are they able to charge their best possible rates. Consumers intuitively gravitate toward exceptional individuals and leaders, and to companies that they believe are exciting, genuine and authoritative.

"Why fit in when you were born to stand out?" – Dr. Seuss

Power Brands keep the world and consumers focused and aligned. Brands are a lens through which we glimpse and shape our reality of the world. Among politics, sports teams, leaders, authors and consumer goods, we look up to and seek trusted brands.

Also, *Power Brands* provide consumers with not only a blanket of security, but also a sense of community. Decades ago, community meant a neighborhood, an alma mater, the local tavern, or a church. And for many of us these remain our cherished brands and connections to our local community.

But the world has become more global and digital. We are now connected on another level with a newer sense of community through social media and mobile devices. These new connections go well beyond our neighborhoods, our religions and our schools. More and more, our communities are being built around social channels, causes and brands, even hashtags.

Branding's primary duty is about creating an experience, a community. Not a transaction.

So, let's define the term *branding*.

"A brand is the set of expectations, memories, stories and relationships that, taken together, account for a consumer's decision to choose one product or service over another." – Seth Godin

"A name, term, design, symbol, or any other feature that identifies one seller's good or service as distinct from those of other sellers. The legal term for brand is trademark. A brand may identify one item, a family of items, or all items of that seller. If used for the firm as a whole, the preferred term is trade name." – American Marketing Association

"The intangible sum of a product's attributes: its name, packaging, and price, its history, its reputation, and the way it's advertised." - David Ogilvy

"A brand is essentially a container for a customer's complete experience with the product or company." - Sergio Zyman

"The art of differentiation." - David Brier

"Your Brand is Your Personality." – Bloomberg *BusinessWeek*

"Your distinctive, indispensable attributes and value." – Edwin Dearborn

The word "brand" comes from the Germanic root *biernan,* meaning, "burn." In commercial-market branding, it is all about product and service attributes that make a lasting impression in a consumer's mind.

Among all these definitions, you may now have a clearer understanding of what a brand is, and what corporate America refers to when speaking about "branding." As we look at the various integral factors that go into a brand, we can see that it goes way beyond logos and taglines. Yet, when most people speak about their branding they refer only to their logo, tagline and packaging, or to promotional items that feature their logo.

BREAKING DOWN MY DEFINITION FURTHER:

"Your Distinctive, Indispensable Attributes and Value."

Distinctive - *"Characteristic of one person or thing, and so serving to distinguish it from others."* In other words, what makes up your character? What are your core beliefs and personal ethos? Your brand must reflect what is genuinely characteristic about you, in that it clearly distinguishes you apart from others.

Indispensable – *"1. Absolutely necessary; essential. 2. Incapable of being disregarded or neglected. 3. A person or thing that is indispensable."* A great brand is something or someone that is considered a "must be associated with, and/or obtained." In someone's life, possessing this brand has to be essential to their survival or quality of life in <u>their</u> estimation.

Attributes – *"1. A quality or feature regarded as a characteristic or inherent part of something or someone. 2. Something used as a symbol of a particular* *person, office or status.*"For example, brands are often defined by a logo (Apple, Starbucks), a certain color (Tiffany & Co.), even a distinctive sound (Harley-Davidson), among other ways.

Value – *"1. The importance, worth, or usefulness of something. 2. Consider someone or something to be important or beneficial; have a high opinion of. 3. Monetary worth of something or someone."* Value is a term often abused by branding professionals and marketers, but the essence of value is the importance people place on something or someone. (More on *Value* in a later chapter.) Your own value is directly proportional to how important you are in the lives of others.

Your branding and content will resonate further and deeper within consumer minds if your brand is founded on the bedrock of thorough market research. As David Ogilvy would put it, "What does the customer think?"

The more you do research into the mind, personal values, thoughts, desires and dreams of your potential customer, the better your brand will resonate and arouse. The fact is, doing good research is easier today for small business owners than at any previous time in American business and marketing history. Resources abound on how to discover what motivates people to associate with and purchase particular brands.

THE BASIC ELEMENTS OF BRANDING

The elements that go into a brand are multi-layered and can develop into quite a complex system. How many companies have been thrown into the waste bin of bankruptcy, which had a great logo? Too many. Successful branding is so much more than the simple possession of a great logo and beautifully printed materials.

THE KEY TANGIBLES

The most important tangibles within the brand identity are the name, design and packaging. Without question, this becomes the brand's most recognizable and unique features. As branding guru David Brier states, "Design is the mysterious 'X factor' that will continue to embrace the public."

From the name of the product or service, its logo, the colors, the packaging and even the design of the actual products that we use each and every day, design plays a vital role in how a brand distinguishes itself above the rapid growth of competitors in today's business world.

Let's dig deeper and select a few key words and concepts from the above definitions and quotes, such as:

* Expectations
* Memories
* Stories
* Relationships
* Attributes
* History
* Reputation
* Experiences
* Value

In large part, these words represent *intangible assets*, such as expectations, memories, reputation and experiences. These are the finer aspects that show up in the way you treat people, render customer service and deliver hospitality; in the tones and the overall ethos of your company, and how you determine and communicate your brand's stories.

More often than not, people purchase experiences rather than things.

Sadly, I have seen too many small business people and entrepreneurs point to their logo, branded water bottle and other tangibles, and assert their expertise about branding their company. Yet, one look into their business sites reveals lackadaisical employees, slow service and unmet expectations. They have not observed that the *intangibles* are also vital components of the consumer's "brand experience."

Believe me, over time, customers pay far more attention to the above intangibles than to a great logo or free water bottles. Too many businesses have not learned that their brand's intangibles are what motivate the consumer's long-term "brand loyalty." **Power Brands** go beyond "great customer service" to render consistent, undeniable, and memorable hospitality.

WHY THE INTANGIBLE IS SO IMPORTANT

Let's try a Yelp restaurant review, for example. How many would go like this: "Their service and food completely sucked, but the logo on the free water bottle they offered me was awesome. Because of their logo, I'm going back."

You won't be seeing that type of review any time soon, because most online reviews are much more about the intangibles, not the brand's tangibles.

"Product distinctions, the historic centerpiece of product marketing, exist only briefly - and in the prospects' minds, often not at all." - Harry Beckwith, *Selling the Invisible: A Field Guide to Modern Marketing*

While it is imperative to excel with the tangible assets of your branding (i.e., logos, colors, materials, website, terms, symbols, price, packaging, location and advertising methods), the battlefield of the intangibles is also where great brands shine above the rest. Don't get me wrong here: it remains that developing and creating unique qualities within these tangibles are necessary and primary steps in building a *Power Brand.*

Recall your most cherished restaurant – the one that you would drive out of your way for just to be there and to drink in the atmosphere and eat the food. Is it their logo that keeps you coming back? No. But, maybe the vibe you feel when you are there, or their friendly service, or their signature dishes are what motivate you to return, right?

Even greasy-spoon diners, branded and managed correctly, project the magic of their intangibles upon their diners and they flourish.

Power Brands have grasped the power of the intangibles. They know this and they leverage this power consistently with panache.

When developing a brand and the tangible assets for your company, it is vitally important that intangibles play a part in your strategy to create and add distinctiveness to your business and its content. How will people be greeted? What is your dress code, if any? How fast will your services or products be delivered? How will you exceed expectations at every touch point? What are *your* key intangibles that you can feature and offer, which will truly distinguish your offer above and beyond from the rest of the pack?

MAKING IMPORTANT PROMISES

A *Power Brand* makes an important promise to its consumers. Creating and fulfilling an expectancy, a higher level of experience or set of experiences is what any ***Power Brand*** must set out to accomplish by accentuating a key promise, a fulfillment or accomplishment that is highly desired, a ***Power Brand*** becomes an indispensable aspect within the lives of consumers. Such promises can be:

- Power
- Prestige
- Peace of mind
- Personal fulfillment
- Solutions
- Better direction in life
- Health
- Membership (belonging)
- Beauty
- Wealth

All the tangibles and intangibles bleed into an effortless harmony, which features, clearly communicates and delivers into the hands of the consumer that accentuated promise.

Tangible + Intangible = The Unimaginable

Try to conceive how Disney pulls off the unimaginable. This is a ***Power Brand*** that goes way beyond the tangible in their branding and service initiatives. There is good reason why we call it the "Magic Kingdom" and know it as "The Happiest Place on Earth." Walt Disney knew, and his successors know, that for branding to take on a life of its own, one must master the intangibles beyond the imaginable norm.

"Disneyland" and other brands were not built solely on logos, great taglines and packaging. Yes, these were, and still remain, vital components within their branding and their continuous marketing efforts; but Disneyland and other cherished brands also deliver intangibles like no other.

Top brands go through excruciating organizational pains; intense internal evaluations, and commitment challenges in the evolutions of the important elements within their brand. They do so to ensure that their brand is genuine, relevant, and consumed well above their competitors' numbers. Great brands conceive of and deliver the unimaginable with every available facet to hand. They own a piece of real estate in just about everyone's mind. And the result is that they become unforgettable, even legendary.

"The new competitive battlefield is not the engine or the air conditioner – it is the design, the warranty, the service deal, the image and the finance package. Intelligence and intangibles. Emotions. And, of course, people. People can make your organization, your products, and your service solutions unique. How you manage and lead people, how you organize your operations, will determine whether or not you succeed." - Kjell Nordstrom and Jonas Ridderstrale, Book: *Funky Business*.

In building your **Power Brand**, all the tangible and intangibles must be proactively engineered into a holistic package. How your **Power Brand** appeals to the physical human senses is crucial, but it must also must touch our minds and hearts, creating a sense of awe.

HERE IS A PRACTICAL EXERCISE YOU CAN DO:

I suggest that you sit down with your fellow branding people, mentors, business coaches and good friends and list out on paper or a monitor screen all of the important tangibles and intangibles that you can associate with your brand, using the list and ideas above. Next, figure out in detail the nuances of how your brand can leverage and feature those tangibles and intangibles to differentiate itself in every possible way.

This may be your most important branding exercise!

As well, study the successful actions of other brands within your niche and/or industry and determine what those are exactly. How can you perform them better, faster, or in a more select manner? Again, you are looking to *differentiate* your products and services on the most important *tangible* and *intangible* factors.

Admittedly, this can become a daunting task. This may be the very point where you need to reach out and acquire the professional help of branding experts, particularly those who have demonstrated branding success within your industry or niche.

You must, in every way possible, distinguish your brand. Famed business expert Peter Drucker remarked, "Marketing is the distinguishing, unique function of the business."

CHAPTER 6

More on Value

❖ ❖ ❖

VALUE defined:

NOUN:

1. The regard that something is held to deserve; the importance, worth, or usefulness of something. 2. A person's principles or standards of behavior; one's judgment of what is important in life.

VERB:

1. Estimate the monetary worth of (something). 2. Consider (someone or something) to be important or beneficial; have a high opinion of

IN MY OPINION, THE WORD *Value* is the most ill-defined and abused word in the field of marketing. I am sure that, to most consumers, this word sounds mildewed and has lost all its punch and gravity. In fact, I call upon you to ask 100 marketers to define the word *value*. I am sure that you will receive a wide variety of answers, most of them shallow and off the mark.

Value = Importance

In short, value represents *what we believe to be important*. For something to be important and of genuine value to us and our lives, it must:

* Align with our core values and principles - good, bad or indifferent.
* Be worth something to us monetarily, as well as for the quality of our lives.
* Be useful; something that fulfills a purpose and/or achieves a goal in our lives.

Value has been debased as a word to represent saved money or to purchase something cheaper than something else. For sure, to some people saving money or purchasing something cheaper *is* the highest value they look for in a particular brand, product or service. Rather than buy Coca-Cola ("The Real Thing"), they are content to purchase the grocery-store brand of cola.

At on the other end of the consumer spectrum are those who would never purchase any cola drink but, instead, would spend $12 for a 16-ounce cup of an organic juice at Whole Foods Market. For them, the perception of drinking something healthy has more value.

These phenomena are why market research is so important and why research needs to be conducted continuously. What we deem valuable (important to us) changes over time, including in particular what we expect from a brand's services, features and perceived benefits.

Ten years ago, gluten-free products were unheard of; now these product lines collectively are a multi-million dollar industry growing by leaps and bounds. Gluten-free items appear regularly on menus in restaurants and in special sections featuring gluten-free products stocked at local grocery stores. There even exist specialty stores, which offer only gluten-free products.

> "A small but growing number of suppliers in business markets draw on their knowledge of what customer's value, and would value, to gain marketplace advantages over their less knowledgeable competitors. These suppliers have developed what we call *customer value models,* which are data-driven representations of the worth, in monetary terms, of what the supplier is doing or could do for its customers." – Harvard Business Review (November 1998)

Often, the *invisible* aspects of life are what represent the most value to people. How one is greeted and treated is incredibly valuable. How your brand interacts with your community, or what it does to help humanity, is a core value for other clientele.

The bottom line is simple: what we consider of value may be complex, simple, common sense, or a delicate issue, and perhaps a combination of several qualities, but *Value* always means that something is important to our lives.

WHAT MAKES *POWER BRANDS AMAZING*

Great brands elevate themselves into the circle of amazing and memorable by completely understanding the meanings of *value* as described and defined. Built intrinsically in a simple but meaningful way, **Power Brands** incorporate unique value propositions without coming across as cheap or offensive. Structured in several layers, they connect with their audience's values in whatever terms apply, including price, beliefs, principles, goals and personal taste, among other significances. Their logo, customer service, content, messaging, touchpoints, products and services come together like a symphony, communicating and resonating with its patrons.

When these factors align, when the presentation of them hits all of the senses... Voila! We have a ***Power Brand*** success!

POWER BRANDS ARE ERGONOMICALLY BUILT

Power Brands know how to capture our hearts and souls. Questions that require introspection and honest answers can lead as power-brand-marketing aids:

* Do you understand what your customers find to be most important to them?
* Have you identified your most important audience in terms of demographics and psychographics?
* Have you surveyed your existing customer base to ensure that you know their unique needs, expectations and goals?
* Is your customer data integrated and easily accessible to your owner and marketing and sales team?
* Are your sales team members regularly consulted to see if shifts in needs and expectations are occurring in the market place?
* Does your staff have access to collected details of information concerning your customers?

ACTIONS TO INITIATE:

* Analyze and summarize the data concerning your customer relationships and potential new markets that you want to acquire.
* Share this data with your Marketing and Sales teams to ensure that they understand this information. Get their feedback on how the data could best be leveraged into your content marketing strategy, as well as in the content itself.

- Develop content that will best resonate with your customers and your potential new markets.
- Distribute this content regularly along the channels best-suited to for your audiences.

How These Actions Will Benefit Brand Value and ROI:

- Marketing and Sales efforts become much more effective and fruitful.
- Knowledgeable employees make decisions more accurately and efficiently, better fulfilling customer needs and demands.
- Your customer's experience strengthens the relationship and mutual communication resonates with truth and actual value realized.
- Employee morale sustained and raised as complaints are addressed better.
- Increased lifetime value and trust derived from your clientele.

When Value Is a Mirror

As best as you can, you want to mirror your client's core values, beliefs and desires with your brand's promise and branded content. Publishing content will be as successful as you resonate and parallel along these lines.

A Word about Price

While cost and price are most definitely something to consider when building a product, there is something else to consider with your branding. We need only look to the example of the retail company Nordstrom, to understand why.

Nordstrom, one of the world's best known, loved, and successful brands, sells their products at higher-than-usual prices. Their ardent followers know full well that they will spend more money there than if they shopped elsewhere.

Nordstrom understands that *price is not the most important **value** to* their loyal legion of fans. Nordstrom made Customer Service their hallmark and they have profited. Their competitors who offered lower prices are closing down stores nationwide.

Like a close and trusted friend, we choose our brands on how well they mirror our values. It only makes sense for companies and brands to emulate their consumers.

CHAPTER 7

The Branding Triangle

❖ ❖ ❖

BRANDING AS AN ACTION TERM can be illustrated, allowing us to clarify how each vital aspect and component of branding dovetails together with the others. Just as an engineer must plan out a bridge before constructing it, so, too, must you prepare your branding strategy before developing and marketing it to your target audience(s).

Power branding extends well beyond the boundaries of what most people in business conceive to be "the all" of branding: the *brand identity*.

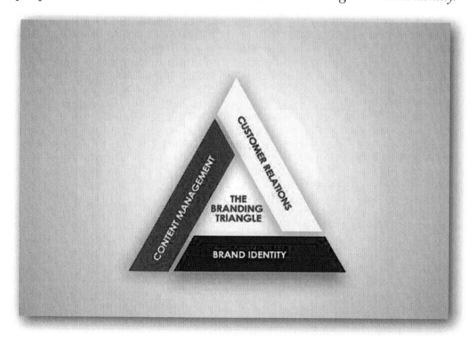

BRAND IDENTITY

The core elements of what we traditionally have referred to as a "brand" are contained within its visible *"brand identity."* The components of the brand identity are created by the business itself. In other words, brand identity is the way in which a business wants its potential consumers to perceive and remember its brand. Brand identity forms an important base within the activity of branding, as this is how we first perceive it, as well as continue to recognize the brand in the future. The brand identity forms the foundation of the Branding Triangle.

Now, how a brand is *actually* perceived by the consumer is different, and referred to as the ***"brand image."***

Within a brand's identity are:

* The logo
* Symbols and icons
* Type style
* Colors
* Packaging
* Store design and decor
* Uniforms
* Art work
* Photography
* Slogan/tag line
* Voice or sounds
* Distinguishing visual/audio elements
* Placement and location

CONTENT MANAGEMENT

Moving in a clockwise manner, the next integral part of the Branding Triangle is Content Management. The administration of your processes, messaging and technologies concerning your *content* is another critical aspect of creating and maintaining the awareness, appreciation of and connections of your customers and followers with your brand. Without the creation and intelligent management of "branded content," your company brand and products and/or services will rapidly become irrelevant and forgotten, even by your most ardent customers and advocates. *"Out of sight, out of mind,"* is the maxim be cognizant of at all times. After the brand establishes its identify, it must communicate and become known.

Consumers no longer want a spec sheet or product description that *tells* them what the product or service is — they want to be *shown* what the product or service can do for them. And they want to see how other actual people — just like them — use the product or service.

A **Power Brand** cannot become or remain one if it is not continuously communicating and connecting with its audience. Due to the fact that the world is becoming more automated, creating personalized content can become a huge differentiator for the **Power Brand** that takes heed of this branding opportunity.

When it comes to **Power Branding**, content management is ultimately the responsibility of the Chief Marketing Officer (CMO) or, in the case of a small business or startup, the owner or Chief Executive Officer (CEO). Your brand, in part, is as vibrant as the content that it publishes and distributes, and the help that it offers. This content may be your images, video and audio properties, sales decks, blogs, eBooks, published materials, emails, newsletters, press releases, tweets, and even the content of your character reflected in your smile.

Effective content management concerns itself with:

1. Market research
2. Brand touch points and execution

3. Content creation
4. Scheduling
5. Editing
6. Publishing and distribution
7. Monitoring consumer and media feedback
8. Audience development (Increasing the number of genuine contacts, fans and followers)
9. Oversight and review
10. Recommendations for future content and PR initiatives

How Content Connects with Branding

Your content forms the second aspect of the Branding Triangle. If your brand is not creating content that shows customers how to do something, you are missing out on a big opportunity to provide customer service in a format that customers increasingly demand and love.

Once you have produced your how-to content, you can share it in a variety of places. Of course, your business website is the primary location to host your content; include it as part of your customer-service page. But also place your videos on your YouTube channel and share the video links to the content throughout your other social-media channels. Done right, how-to content keeps existing customers happy and attracts new ones, too.

It is content that initiates and continues the relations and decisions to purchase from your ***Power Brand.*** It is your content that creates curiosity and builds trust. Content accomplishes this by exposing your audiences to the conditions that the ***Power Brand*** is resolving, thus deepening awareness of how important that ***Power Brand*** is to their survival and happiness.

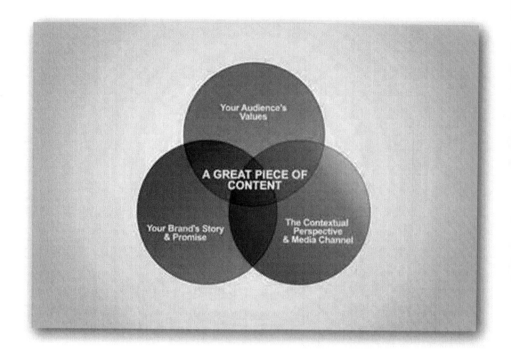

Customer Relationship Management

(Customer relations management and "customer service" are interchangeable depending on the industry and their preferred nomenclature.)

The third corner of the Branding Triangle traditionally has not been considered among most branding-professionals' circles. The fact remains, however, that any brand is only valued and regarded well to the degree that it renders *service to its consumers* and successfully grows the brand's relationship with every interaction and touch point. This is where "brand *identity*" (How a brand *desires* to be perceived.) and "brand *image*" (How consumers *actually* perceive it.) begin to bridge the chasm between strategy and reality.

How to deliver *more than* the most fundamental customer expectancies within a brand's services and touch points ought to be included within any integral strategic planning, when creating and marketing a brand. *Exceeding* your customers' expectations is a sure route to establishing a **Power Brand.**

"When it comes to brand building, customer service is often the last and most-ignored piece of the puzzle. This is a big mistake – and big missed opportunity. Aligning customer service and your brand is an essential but under-used way to attract and retain customers, differentiate the business, and boost brand loyalty. Done right, it can create a truly sustainable competitive advantage." - Harvard Business Review (April 6, 2009)

While it is your brand identity that will initially attract new clients, it is customer service – a brand image intangible – that determines whether they stick around or leave. With the advent of online consumer reviews, the quality of your customer service is even more important today. The manner in which you service your customers is as vital to your business' future existence as breathing.

CUSTOMER SERVICE

Power Brands create loyal customers by helping them solve their problems quickly and easily, even anticipating their problems for them. *"Get it right the first time,"* is the Golden Rule, but efficient delivery of *more than* what the customer expects is branding platinum!

Speedy, efficient service trumps "being delightful," which seems to be the current trend around customer-service circles. While, of course, I always advocate for friendly service at all times, if service is slow and inefficient, no amount of friendliness is going to compensate or ease a customer's complaints. Citing an analogous example that many of us are familiar with, the frustrating pain of waiting five hours at the Department of Motor Vehicles (DMV) – no one's idea of a pleasant day at the office – will not be mitigated by how friendly their staff are when your number is finally called.

"Making promises and keeping them is a great way to build a brand." – Seth Godin

When it comes to customer service, *Power Brands* are:

* Fast
* Efficient
* Solution oriented

STAGE MANAGE THE CUSTOMER EXPERIENCE

In the eyes of your customer, your *Power Brand* will always be in the spotlight. And like a Broadway musical, you need to practice good stage management so that your performance is flawless and consistent.

Establishing and enforcing known policies and business processes allows a *Power Brand* to become so well rehearsed, that employees are able to focus their full attention and care unto your customers, not confusions or disorganized work spaces.

POWER BRANDS DILIGENTLY MANAGE THE TRIANGLE

When all three major elements of a brand come together within a business, they have established the firmest foundation for real *Power Brand* success. Case in point, again, is Disneyland. Before the park opened in July of 1955, the brand of Disney Studios, which began in 1923, was well-established. Creating content with films and iconic characters had built that brand decades before Disney created a theme park.

After the park opened, more movie characters created in following decades began to shape the theme park's new rides and attractions. Eventually, these affected Disney's current swag.

Anyone who has visited Disneyland has benefited from the highly attentive customer service found at the "Happiest Place on Earth."

And they have witnessed and experienced the perfect blend of the Branding Triangle.

Power Branding truly is *"the aggregate of all tangibles and intangibles."*

CHAPTER 8

TRUST

BRANDING'S MOST IMPORTANT INTANGIBLE IS trust.

The Holy Grail of branding, marketing and PR is *earned trust*. Before consumers spend any money, some element of trust must be established. In the beginning, that trust is fragile at best, resting on a hope that you will deliver the same or better of quality that you have promoted and offered. If you meet consumer expectations, more than likely you will maintain that trust and, importantly, their continued business. However, if you exceed their expectations, you will certainly build upon and expand that initial trust, as well as generate positive word of mouth and online reviews, leading to even more business.

Of course, not meeting their expectations, you will not earn their trust. Your brand may even earn some negative reviews, if not jail time, as in the case of taking their money without any expectation of delivering something in return, which, of course, is criminal.

"Consumers today have many options, and more than ever they choose particular brands to communicate something personal about their own beliefs and priorities. The best way to establish and reinforce common values is to create content that's so highly specific it defines not only the brand, but the customer." - Harvard Business Review

To earn **Power Brand** status a company must exert control over their messaging, content, quality of service and product. By doing so, they proactively create a culture of trust. While people's feelings or the economic environment cannot be managed, one can manage policies, content and service ethic, and leave people with a feeling of appreciation, understanding, community and transparency. These are the managed components that reduce risk in the mind of the consumers, which will also elevate trust with your power brand.

Power Brands appreciate and embrace this trust factor. By proactively building all of their strategies, content, employee training, business processes, as well as conducting themselves in ways intended to build and maintain people's trust. Satisfaction grows and positive reviews begin to populate across the Web. The trust factor builds exponentially, and sales and income returns soar.

POWER BRANDING FOR SMALL BUSINESS

One of my personal gripes concerning books that tout branding and marketing is that the only examples presented are Fortune 500 types. Admittedly, I am guilty of promoting this way to some degree as well, but these books offer no real model to emulate for 98 percent of the small and medium businesses that are looking to improve their branding.

If you were to select a brand that you frequent, such as your local coffee shop, your CPA or dentist, or maybe even your dry cleaner, you could observe and compare their branding efforts against the three distinct elements of the Branding Triangle, as described earlier.

While their brand identity may be important to you, I am sure that their content and friendly, efficient service is more important to you as a consumer.

For a coffee house, content is the quality of their menu selection - the coffee, and keeping you abreast of any entertainment events that they may feature. My favorite coffee house, The Lost Bean in Tustin, CA, has a simple and unique branding position: all of their featured coffees are organically grown. While their brand identity is important to me, I can assure you that if the coffee tasted like hell, or if they took 10 minutes to serve me my coffee, they would lose my business. Since all three elements of power branding are in evidence at The Lost Bean, I regularly frequent the place. They have a unique brand identity, offer relatively fast customer service and their content (the coffee and food) is tasty and worthy of my consumption and sharing.

The Lost Bean's primary marketing strategy includes offering a 10% discount every time their customers check in on Facebook or Yelp. This builds positive reviews and continues to grow their followers for use to announce more events and promote new menu items.

Peer-to-peer online reviews are powerful content for small business places like The Lost Bean, and email still represents an important distribution channel for their branded content.

"Companies with better reputations tend to do better financially when there are downturns in the market even though everyone may go down. Companies with good reputations bounce back more quickly. They tend to recruit and keep the best people. They tend to lower their cost of capital, so there are some real bottom-line implications for a CEO or others on why reputations are really important." - LeBow College of Business

Brand Touchpoints and Execution

Once research is complete, you need to determine which brand touch-points will interact best with your customers. At first, this appears obvious. The customer will see your logo, tagline, website, videos and business cards. But additional touchpoints exist, which are not obvious on first look. For instance, how your front-office personnel answer the phone is a touchpoint. Your tweets and the tone of each message are touchpoints. The aggregate, correct use of all possible touchpoints might be the difference between your brand winding up as a loser and someone else's winning the battle for consumer minds.

Truthfully, there is so much more to consider when you are planning your marketing strategically for power branding. The grouping of such data is referred to as *Brand Development Strategy* (BDS).

The Cultural Impasse within Branding

Business leaders today, who have sweated in boardroom trenches, burned through many midnight oil lamps past hundreds of sunrises, and built memorable brands and power-branded organizations over the last 20 to 30 years, are still scratching their heads in wonderment, trying to figure out how to market to younger consumers who have grown up in our digital age.

In the past, a brand's community was built around school, the local neighborhood and one's general area of business. But social media has more than turned the tables on that limited era.

Now the sense of and connection to community is much more complex, albeit more dynamic.

Social-media advances have left many corporations, nonprofits, and entire nations, small and large, in a shockwave, because younger people rapidly connect and communicate their ideas globally without any third-party meddling or involvement. Social media has forever changed the playing field and is altering the rules almost every day as it evolves.

This presents a new conundrum for traditional branding and marketing mindsets. Their old paradigms and familiar base models no longer fit the mold, if indeed, there are molds to follow today. Everything is moving so fast. And brand loyalty is harder to build and retain because social transparency has become, well, painfully transparent.

Beneath the changes, however, understanding how to connect with a targeted audience's "branding neurons" remains, like before, a process of discovering common topics that can be discussed, in which agreement can be found. Topics for social-media agreement can be about a person, a place, a sports team, a cause, a food item, or even God himself.

Once we establish the topic of discussion that hits an agreeable nerve, we have to establish the guiding philosophy, belief or set of ideals that characterize that community. And that brings us to how these ideals are to be presented by words, images, videos, songs and activities; who we support within our network; what goals we are committed to; and a myriad of other items that will help us identify what the brand is about, if we want to belong, or, at least, participate as a consumer.

ANCIENT GREECE AND MODERN BRANDING
Power Brand creation is about creating what the ancient Greeks called *Eunoia*, (you-no-ya) defined as, "The goodwill a speaker cultivates between himself and his audience, a condition of receptivity." The derivation of the word helps us understand this uncommon word:

(*eúnoia*, "goodwill", literally "beautiful thinking"), from εὖ (*eû*, "well, good") + νόος (*nóos*, "mind, spirit").

Eunoia, quite appropriate to our discussion concerning branding and brand content, is built upon a genuine discussion and an authentic trajectory of message, which elicits empathy and cooperation between marketers and consumers.

Brand-building should no longer be built on egotism, but, instead, upon discussions of beliefs that build eúnoia. The modern tools are two-way communication and empathy. Egotism does not possess capacity for empathy – a luxury, really. Nor does the egotist care to help elevate people and help them to learn and become enlightened.

Self-centered brands are old-fashioned, an all-but-dead relic of the pre-digital marketing age.

A recent analysis published by the World Advertising Research Centre of nearly 880 case studies found that advertising campaigns focused on emotional engagement tend to be more profitable than those focused on rational messages (Low prices, special offers, etc.), even when times are tough.

The empathetic brands of today celebrate and encourage their audiences to be interactive, getting them to help guide the direction of the brand's message. They even let their prospects and customers participate in the ideation and creation of their branded content. Versus fearing and trying to manipulate the thoughts of today's targeted audiences, *Power Brands* have learned to resonate and participate with their audience's needs, ideas, messages, participation, advocacy, and creativity.

They understand eúnoia.

THE NO. 1 ENEMY OF EFFECTIVE BRANDING

Someone new to branding or is not well-versed in branding, usually gravitates toward the cliché because they believe that this is branding and marketing. But, now you know better.

The most obvious fault with clichés is that they are boring; everyone is saying the exact same thing. And your bored, target audience drowns it all out.

Now let me ask you a question: does sounding the same as your competitor fit the earlier mentioned definitions of branding? Not at all. Being the same equates to boring, and boring doesn't sell.

"Imitation is suicide."- Ralph Waldo Emerson

If you intend for your branding to be truly unique, every aspect of your branding, even just slightly, must be unique. There has to be something perceptively distinctive about your brand—the elusive "It" quality sought after for notoriety, acclaim and financial success. Even the broker of a nationwide brand operating from his office on a street corner, who is selling the same insurance plans as everyone else in town, needs to find his unique angle, his bit of flair and undisputed niche or customer-service point that is going to make his or her *brand image* stand out.

Common Clichés in Branding:

- Best in class
- World-class service
- Cutting edge
- State of the art
- Innovative

- One-stop shop
- Highest quality
- Lowest price
- Once in a lifetime
- Discover the difference
- Revolutionary
- We do it all
- We treat you like family

How you sound, how you look, how you communicate makes you stand out, or not. The dress or suit and the colors that you wear, to whom you direct your messages, and how you service people… whatever these are for you and your business you need to figure these out. And then you need to be or do it better than any of your competitors…with one caveat.

THE NO. 1 BRAND MYTH: "BE THE BEST"

A big myth in branding, that one has to be the best (*"Numero uno baby!"*) within your industry, is a brand-marketing LIE. If being the best is what you have in mind naturally, so be it. I am not one to lower anyone's ambition. But reality tells us that you can absolutely become a multi-millionaire, world famous, and have millions of ardent fans by being #75 in your industry.

Case in point: The Eagles.

According to *Rolling Stone* magazine, The Eagles are ranked 75th among "the greatest musical artists of all time." Now, while some of their avid fans would find disfavor with the ranking, let's take a look at their brand and their many achievements, despite 75th place among their peers:

- The Eagles have sold over 150 million albums.
- They are the fifth-highest-selling music act and highest-selling American band in U.S. history.
- No American band has sold more records than the Eagles did during the 1970's.
- Five No. 1 singles.
- Six Grammys.
- Five American Music Awards.
- Six No. 1 albums.
- Inducted into the Rock & Roll Hall of Fame in 1998.
- The Recording Industry of America (RIAA) honored the group with Best Selling Album of the Century for *Their Greatest Hits (1971–1975).*
- Helped launch the successful, individual, musical careers of three band members: Don Henley, Glenn Frey and Joe Walsh.

Between you and me, many a band, past or present, could find much satisfaction with these achievements and being considered in "just" 75th place.

Here's the point: your brand can face a highly competitive environment and still carve out a large-enough, dedicated audience that can carry you to great financial success and epic achievement.

PRICING AND BRAND STRATEGY

In an earlier chapter, I touched upon pricing as a branding tactic. It deserves more attention here.

By itself, your pricing cannot become your *Power Brand* strategy. Because if your brand strategy and position is to have the lowest price, it is just a matter of time before someone comes around and cuts that price even lower. Just ask K-Mart what happened the day that Wal-Mart opened its doors. And how Wal-Mart executives felt when Target decided to compete against them.

When a business like Wal-Mart operates with the "lowest price" brand strategy, they are operating on almost no profit margin. Yet, low-price strategy is the go-to visceral reaction for too many entrepreneurs and small businesses, particularly when sales slow down or competition becomes more pronounced.

Earlier in this book, we defined *value*. The words *cheap, inexpensive* or *lowest price* are nowhere to be found in its definition. Still, more than a century of incessant, dull-witted advertising, and a constant inculcation of bad branding, have made the word *value* synonymous with these lesser words. We have become brainwashed by Madison Avenue and the work of cheap marketeers into believing that value means low price.

Value is what we as consumers consider and deem to be important. And tens of millions of people do not consider lowest price important. Were it so, no one would wait in line for 10 minutes at Starbucks or Peet's Coffee & Tea to get their five-dollar, custom, caffeinated concoctions. Nor would there be millions of Mercedes-Benz's roaming the highways of the world and Nordstrom would be empty of customers.

Power Brands want to be fair with pricing, but profitable, too. Whatever your targeted audiences want... power, convenience, prestige, peace of mind, freedom, a sense of rebellion, of belonging to some important cause, personal security, family values, elation, or other emotional factors; whatever *your* customers deem extremely important in their lives is what you need to represent, promote and deliver.

You must strategically position your brand in the mind of your target audience as *the* brand of choice because only a **Power Brand** confers an important quality, a genuine emotional connection; access to a more ideal lifestyle for your customers.

CHAPTER 9

What Is Branded Content?

WHAT POSITIONS ONE BRAND AS an authority in a field that possesses many options? Quite often what separates a brand above the crowd is their Branded Content.

There are many colleges and universities but only a handful are regarded as authorities in their field. Harvard, publisher of the *Harvard Business Review*, comes to mind easily. There are several talk-show hosts, but Oprah Winfrey also publishes a blog and a printed magazine. There are thousands of authors, but only a handful also do public speaking, write books, as well as blog on a daily basis, like Seth Godin.

Authorities are known as such because of the body of work that they produce: their branded content.

It should be your intention to make your Branded Content become one of your most valuable strategic assets to differentiate you from all of the other noise and alternatives in your chosen marketplace.

"Branded Content is any content that can be associated with a brand in the eye of the beholder." - Branded Content Marketing Association (BCMA)

Organizations that create and distributing Branded Content are nothing new to the business world. However, the advancement of technology, particularly the evolution and usage of social media, makes the process of content creation and dissemination much easier. This is particularly true for consumer-generated content such as online reviews. Likewise, social media, followed by the advent of millions of apps and hundreds of millions of mobile devices in use around the globe, have eased the consumption of Branded Content.

The best way for any brand to reach and influence its target audience, thus instigating positive attention and buzz, is by creating and distributing engaging Branded Content. Great content can elevate any brand to a high level of prestige and authority.

Branded Content pushes out in numerous forms, including advertiser-funded programming, videos, events, blogs, eBooks, eCourses and webinars, among others. It comes, therefore, as no surprise that the term "Branded Content" possesses different meanings to different people, easily leading to misunderstandings and confusion.

"Traditional advertising is about delivering features, benefits, and a USP through a product story, and then finding creative ways to connect that to people. Branded Content is sort of the reverse of this. It's about starting with people stories first, so what are the things that can help brands connect with the hearts and minds of their audience, and then thinking about how you can creatively link that to your product." - Avi Savar, founder of Big Fuel

Here are three examples of small businesses succeeding with great Branded Content.

Foiled Cupcakes never had a storefront, but they surpassed their revenue goals by 600 percent because they delivered amazing service on Twitter (@foiledcupcakes) and blogged religiously (foiledcupcakes. com/blog). Mari Luangrath started her online cupcake-ordering business in 2009. But she had a problem: her website didn't work. For the first six weeks no one could order cupcakes. Instead of taking the loss, she went to Twitter and started chatting. Foiled Cupcakes grew from zero customers to 2,200 targeted followers in less than 6 weeks, attracted national press, and beat their sales targets by 600 percent!

River Pools and Spas avoided going out of business during the recession by cutting their traditional marketing budget and focusing on inbound marketing with Branded Content. Business owner Marcus Sheridan faced a challenge: who buys pools in an economic crisis? He realized he needed to become the thought leader for the "inground swimming pool industry," so he started to create and distribute Branded Content, slashing his budget from $150,000 on radio ads, the Yellow Pages and direct mail to $50,000 on inbound marketing. While many of his competitors suffered losses or went out of business, his website traffic increased 300-400 percent, and his leads increased over 400 percent.

Orabrush sells tongue cleaners. Tongue cleaners are not sexy. They had been around for 10 years, trying to convince dentists and retailers to carry their products with limited success before they took off after launching a $500 video. They invested in television advertising and traditional marketing without getting any traction. Then they realized they could create humor around their brand, so they spent $500 on production of a "Bad Breath Test" video that promoted their tongue cleaner. They posted it on YouTube. To date, the Orabrush channel has had over 40 million views, and attracted 340,000+ Facebook fans and 5,000+ Twitter followers. After 10 years, major drugstore chains finally carry Orabrush.

Branded Content is no longer solely for large corporations or developed exclusively by media agencies on Madison Avenue. The small business person and entrepreneur who sees that in today's digital age that Branded Content works, can be highly effective and profitable. Of course, this must be conducted intelligently, particularly when on a small budget.

BRANDED CONTENT MUST BE CONTEXTUAL

You must, must, must get your wits around the term *context!* While content is absolutely the king, that king sits on the throne of CONTEXT

The formal definition of *context* is, "The circumstances that form the setting for an event, statement, or idea, and in terms of which it can be fully understood and assessed." There is, however, a simpler, more pragmatic definition to grasp and implement in all of your Branded Content. Ask yourself these two questions:

What is my customer thinking? … and

What needs does he or she want fulfilled?

Contextual Branded Content that answers those two important questions fulfills your audience's deepest desires by providing information that specifically meets their needs and wants. When you fulfill those needs, audience delight blossoms.

BRANDED CONTENT INFLUENCING SALES

If each and every one of us could possess a crystal ball and know with certainty what motivates our target audience to buy, we would all surely be millionaires. When Google published their *Zero Moment of Truth* report – the Zero Moment of Truth: **"that invisible moment when a consumer makes a crucial decision about a brand."** – we all moved a little closer toward that ideal.

When and where that mystical moment occurs has been the subject of much guess work and investigation by market-research experts. Factually, it can happen anywhere, at any time and through multiple influences and channels of media. It may be a result of a series of submoments, which germinate at one big moment, when the inquisitive mind converts to a purchaser or an enthusiastic brand advocate.

Here are key takeaways from that ZMOT study:

* 84% of buyers engage in Zero Moment Activities (i.e., online information/education).
* 10.4 Pieces of information are in the buyer's journey prior to purchasing.
* The least-effective action was a following a brand on social media.
* Friends and family, and online reviews are *the* key ZMOT factors.

The ZMOT is the new way of stating that word-of-mouth is critical to how a brand is perceived and, ultimately, consumed. Online Branded Content and brand advocates have become much more important in the buyer's journey.

The ZMOT Report leads to two important considerations:

1. Are you creating a great deal of Branded Content?
2. Are you instigating the sharing of your Branded Content among your followers?

MOST PEOPLE ARE SOLD BEFORE THEY SEE YOU

A Forrester study also confirmed this shift in consumer habits, finding that, on average, prospective customers are more than 70 percent through the sales cycle *prior to* engaging with a brand. This finding indicates a fundamental shift of momentous proportion that can no longer be ignored by large brands, small business owners and entrepreneurs.

According to Gartner Research, by 2020, customers will manage 85% of their buying relationship without ever talking to a human, indicating that future decision makers will count on Branded Content more than ever.

"If you have a company right now, you need to be producing content. Period. Every company is a media company; I've been saying it for years, and it is happening now. So don't get left behind. Make great content, and you'll see the results, I promise." – Gary Vaynerchuk

Creating and sharing content is no longer optional, if one seeks to flourish in business. A few years ago, featuring your basic website was enough to make a difference. Unfortunately, most websites are now seen and used as "online brochures."

Oddly, I still find websites that do not even have a FAQ page to answer their consumer's most common questions, or a simple two-minute video that gives an overview of the company and the values it offers its prospective customers.

How will create Branded Content to differentiate your brand?

CHAPTER 10

Blogging as Branded Content

BLOGGING REPRESENTS ONE OF YOUR best branded content and SEO opportunities, particularly for small business owners and entrepreneurs operating on very tight budgets.

I explain to people and companies new to blogging the following: Your blog is your newspaper; your posts are your published articles, your newspaper content.

"A blog (a truncation of the expression *web log*) is a discussion or informational site published on the World Wide Web and consisting of discrete entries ('posts') typically displayed in reverse chronological order (the most recent post appears first). *Blog* can also be used as a verb, meaning *to maintain or add content to a blog*." – Wikipedia

The advantages of maintaining an active blog are numerous, as you will discover the more you publish posts. Having written over 350 blog articles, I can tell you that without my blog I would not be writing this book. Much of the content in this book derives from my blog.

If I told you to write a 50,000 word book, you'd probably faint. But what if you wrote one-hundred, 500-word blog posts over the next year or so. Blogging can lead to book authorship and its benefits. (More on that later.)

My blogging opened the door for me to experience, at times, the crushing pain and exquisite joys of writing. Blogging also separated and positioned me as the "go to" guy for the right answers and advice on how to conduct correct branding and marketing performances. My articles have led me to new clients, to speaking engagements, and to memberships on Boards of Directors of national brands.

So yes, my blogging has opened the door to many business opportunities.

Companies that blog successfully see an increase in search traffic. A good blog contains fresh and frequently updated content. Such a blog also correctly uses categories and tags to create topical associations; i.e., a local blog's categories might be *city name News, city name Business, city name Events,* and so forth — that's a very SEO-friendly structure. A good blog posts regularly and also receives inbound links regularly.

Good blogs are effective SEO machines. They are link magnets for local marketing and branding purposes. Here are some of the distinct advantages to consistent blogging:

- Blogging allows you to add more content to your website without adding too many unique pages on your website, avoiding clutter and potential audience confusion.
- For SEO purposes, blogging is an amazing way to rank on search engines for very specific long-tail phrases. (Longtail: longer and more specific keyword phrases that visitors are more likely to use when they're closer to a point-of-purchase. Example: "Used Ford F-150 trucks" versus "Ford trucks.") Since each blog post is a unique web page, you can leverage your blog to rank high in search engines for literally hundreds and hundreds of specific keywords and long tails.

* Blogging offers readers fresh, ongoing content, and gives your customers reasons to return and to share your content with others.
* Blogging with consistent, fresh, on-point content, positions you as a key opinion leader — someone to turn to for answers, information and resources, leading, of course, to more customers and sales.
* Blogging allows reach to new markets and broader audiences. Again, guest-blogging works two ways: 1. By your offers for other bloggers to write on your blog, they become more than willing to feature their post to their social media channels to entertain and inform their audiences; 2. By guest blogging on others' blogs, you can reach more people, their audiences, in similar fashion.

BLOGGING AS YOUR COMPETITIVE EDGE

Blogging puts your brand well ahead of your competitors. Why? *Because the majority of your competitors do not blog effectively!*

How many competitors do you think there are, who are located in your county or which share your niche? Probably hundreds, if not thousands, right? And how many would love to have an additional dozen or more high-paying clients per month?

Most likely all of them, right?

But... read this closely... here's the good news: Most marketers today are **not** taking advantage of blogging as a method for reaching the literally millions of searchers *per month,* looking to discover branded services and products that may be just like yours.

"Consumers trust bloggers for a few reasons. First, bloggers are not a company mouthpiece, so the public assumes they are naturally less biased and more honest than a brand's advertisements, website, PR team, CEO, or even employees. Second, bloggers gain their credibility by providing honest opinions and insight into their lives and experiences. Once they start appearing to be 'bought out' they risk losing their audience; so they make efforts to maintain their honesty and authenticity. Third, individuals relate to bloggers on a personal level. They read blogs by individuals who are similar to them and they see themselves in that blogger or aspire to be like that blogger." - Forbes

The branding and marketing advantage in front of you is too good to pass up, or to not optimize for reaching those consumers who are searching for meaningful content.

How to Optimize Your Blog Posts

* Write your blog on a Wordpress format. (There are other platforms available, but this is my preference.)
* Install the Wordpress SEO plugin from Yoast.com. They have a free version that is awesome. This will help you to craft more "SEO friendly" posts.
* Follow the optimization guides from Yoast on how to best optimize each and every blog system. The instructions are easy to follow and provide you with guidance on all factors necessary to optimize a blog post.
* Write killer titles that incorporate the keywords and/or long tails that you want optimized. (This is why keyword research is so vital here.) For example, if the key phrase you want to rank for is "Los Angeles life coach", then your title could be, "Los Angeles Life Coach Offers 7 Tips for Self-Confidence."

- Ensure your blog header images are appealing and grab the eye, so they'll look good in a social media post.
- Make all of your shareable links in Bitly.com format to make your content social media friendly.
- Include a social-share toolbar within your business' blog pages. This can increase the distribution of your content by up to 700 percent.
- Share your articles directly with key influencers. Better yet, quote them in your blog post and tweet to them directly: "Here's my newest blog article, in which you're featured..."
- Comment on an influencer's blog. Be insightful and intelligent, not just flattering.
- Send your best articles posted that week to your email list. Email still represents your best venue to put your blog's content in front of people.
- Do not fear tweeting your content more than once. You can mix up the calls to actions and information in each tweet to make them look unique, yet link back to the same post. This way, new followers will have a chance to see older content.
- Read books and blogs about blogging, if you really find yourself loving it and wanting to excel as a blogger.

Should Your Next Employee Be A Blogger?

"There is no need for advertisements to look like advertisements. If you make them look like editorial pages, you will attract about 50 per cent more readers." – David Ogilvy

The very first reaction I get when I tell a small business owner how much content they should be generating is, "I'm too busy to do that."

Most of them are completely correct: who really has the time to write two to three blog posts per week?

Most business owners are overwhelmed by existing workloads and incomplete tasks, which begs the question, "Could a blogger be your next hire?" The answer is: even if outsourced to a part-time writer, a competitive edge within your area or even your entire industry would be your gain.

There are plenty of retired journalists or journalism students at local universities, who are quite adept at writing and telling a great story. Costs can vary, but blog articles can range from $50 to $200 per article, depending on the subject matter, length and expertise required. For less than a thousand dollars a month, or even for as little as a few hundred dollars per month, you could be creating and distributing great content that engages readers and drives inbound leads from those searching for what you have to offer.

While we all know that any small business would engage in this best SEO and marketing format to generate more customers and revenue, what may not be appreciated is that a competent blogger just might be the most effective addition to your branding-marketing team.

Numerous studies show that inbound marketing through blogging is the most cost-effective way to generate new leads and paying customers. Even if you only hire a part-time blogger, who generates two to three blog posts per week, this strategy can generate 77 percent more inbound leads in a mere matter of a few months, per research conducted by HubSpot.

OPTIMIZING YOUR BRANDED CONTENT

Respected marketing leader, Neil Patel, states on his blog, "If you are trying to grow your qualified search traffic, you have to combine your content marketing with your SEO efforts." To do that, you'll first need to isolate the keywords that are driving the most traffic to your website, as well as those you aren't currently targeting that have the potential to generate more visitors. Once you've identified these phrases, build high quality content around them – content so good 'that even Wikipedia would love to link to."

It's a time-consuming process, sure, but one that stands to benefit your company from both a content marketing and SEO perspective. SEO isn't a single method of driving traffic to a website. SEO is a synthesis of activities working together to accomplish a singular result.

Search Engine Land defines search engine optimization as "the process of getting traffic from the 'free,' 'organic,' 'editorial' or 'natural' listings on search engines."

SEO is not about getting traffic on a single web page or using one single method to increase rankings; rather, it's a strategy that dovetails many important marketing actions. SEO is about doing all that we can to *impress* search engines... as an audience. And we need to show all of our audiences, including Search Engines, that we are committed to servicing their needs with on-point and relevant content.

Whether you do it yourself or you hire a part-time writer, blogging is here to stay. And blogging IS *the* most wide-ranging foundation upon which to reach and engage all of your audiences with high-quality, branded content.

CHAPTER 11

Making Content Work for the Sales Team

❖ ❖ ❖

As THE FOLLOWING INFOGRAPHIC INDICATES, the buyer's journey is easily facilitated when Branding and Marketing work in tandem with the organization's Sales. While this is more often accommodated within large companies, the infographic points to a seamless branding, marketing and sales strategy where Branded Content helps to create a ZMOT connection at the middle.

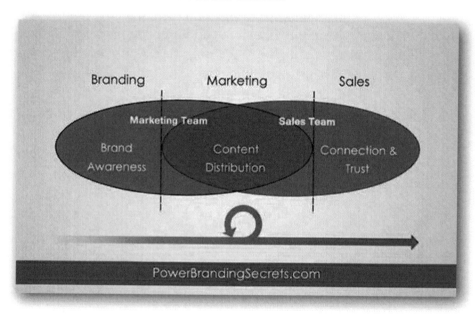

In other words, you want to completely control the story of your brand, its entire content, and, therefore, the sales-funnel journey for your prospective consumers.

Companies not creating easily accessible content in the form of blogs, videos, reports, infographics, brochures, e-Courses, eBooks, consumer reviews and more are missing the content "tasty icing in the middle" that connects Marketing with Sales. Content must be entertaining, insightful, enlightening and motivating enough to prospective customers to move them along the buyer's pathway that the company wishes them to follow.

Prospective buyers are satisfying their interests and questions somewhere, and those resources may be the online reviewer, an influential blogger, a YouTube celebrity, or the content that you create. Guess which one you completely control?

Brands waiting for their sales force to consistently meet quotas without generating Branded Content online and in printed content are missing an increasingly important opportunity to engage their prospects at the critical early stages of their buying pathway.

BRANDED CONTENT: A POWERFUL SALES TOOL

No longer can sales flourish without the support of intelligent, engaging Branded Content. Omitting this type of relevant content you cannot truly support your brand, or render to your salespeople anxious, educated, emotionally involved and desirous prospects. Today's and tomorrow's consumer knows that he or she can access voluminous amounts of information before committing hard-earned pay to any brand.

The companies that understand this epoch-making shift in how buyers look at and investigate brands will recognize why they should change their strategies. They will generate Branded Content as a means for becoming more involved and engaged in proactively creating those zero moments of truth.

To become a **Power Brand** your company must empower both the consumer and your sales professionals with top-notch Branded Content.

THE FORGOTTEN CONTENT

Are you creating content intended for your sales team and employees as part of your branding and marketing strategy? Probably not. The majority of small businesses, and even some major brands, neglect to create exclusive content for their employees and sales teams.

Content created specifically to brief and train your employees is what I refer to as the "forgotten content." The majority of brands, when they do create content, do so solely for their consumers. Realize that your best brand ambassadors are your employees. Brands need content such as company newsletters, training materials, courses, staff events and briefings to help stay abreast of your brand's mission statement, policies, procedures, and accomplishments.

Highly trained and briefed employees become more passionate about the brand that they represent and serve. The employee's feeling of pride and passion rapidly transfers from to your customers. Customers can tell when employees are motivated and happy to work for their brand. Additionally, they also notice when they are not passionate about their own brand.

Creating Branded Content to be specifically seen and consumed by your employees demonstrates to them that you care about their work, their views, and their efforts to create a better work environment for all and a better experience for your customers.

A NOTE ON CONSUMER PURCHASING BEHAVIOR

While your Sales department has to go out there and hustle on a 24/7 basis to sell, we can be realistic about consumer behavior. Common sense tells Sales to keep the sales funnel filled to remain profitable, but there are ebbs and flows in sales. There are annual ebbs and flows, and those that tend to fluctuate with the rise and fall of economies. While never an excuse to not market or sell effectively, these trends create predictable patterns that Marketing and Sales can plan for and flourish through, despite this statistical fact of life.

Unfortunately, most brands are reactionary to seasonal shifts, economic patterns and general movements among consumer sentiments. But veteran and courageous sailors know that, although one can never control the winds, the weather or the tides, one can learn how to pass through treacherous waters, navigate by the stars, and predict inclement weather. Although Old Man Sea takes some of the best sailors to Davey Jones' locker, many more die from lack of plying the waters at all.

Power Brands can also suffer a fate similar to that of the "old salts" of the sea. At best, only one-half of the factors in business life are controllable. The trick is to determine what you can control, and then control that with energetic, consistent planning and action. Preparation, study, vigilance, knowing how to operate one's equipment effortlessly, and trusting one's sixth sense — these are the qualities of a great sailor and a *Power Brand.*

Business, economies and the patterns of society are like seasons. They change and bring sunshine, as well as storms and hurricanes. Batten down the hatches, full speed ahead!

CHAPTER 12

What Is Content Marketing?

IN THE LAST FEW YEARS, there has been quite a bit of buzz concerning content marketing, what it is and how it is properly leveraged by brands.

> "Content marketing is a marketing technique of creating and distributing relevant and valuable content to attract, acquire, and engage a clearly defined and understood target audience – with the objective of driving profitable customer action." - Joe Pulizzi, Content Marketing Institute

Let's break down this simple definition further. The first requisite is to create any content. There are over 50, creatable types of content. (edwindearborn.com/types-of-content/)   The most common are blog posts, videos, eBooks, case studies, press releases, white papers, events, manuals, brochures, webinars, Tweets, and customer reviews. But, as you will see, there is much more content that one can create and distribute.

The second aspect of this definition is "distribution." Factually, you will need to spend just as much time building distribution channels and utilizing them as you do creating your content.

One can create massive amounts of top-end content and still go wanting for new-customer attention. Content is the THING, and

Distribution is GETTING THAT THING INTO THE MINDS AND HANDS OF ANOTHER OR OTHERS. Content *distribution* strategies can be what separates you from competitors, because content never found remains in a non-existent state, and so does your company along with it!

Content marketing strategy breaks down into two broad actions:

1. Creating branded content
2. Distributing branded content

As a marketing strategist working with several companies and industries, I have observed where content creating and content distribution were confused or not given the proper estimation of effort.

- Some people believe that Twitter is content. No, Twitter is a distribution channel. A Tweet is content.
- YouTube is a channel. Your video on YouTube is the content.

A blog can be a channel and it can be the content, depending on which definition you are using. "I have a blog" versus "I just wrote and published my blog post."

A great example is Colgate's website, which features articles that help educate you about oral and dental health. Instead of directly promoting its toothpaste products, the articles focus on topics that people are searching for and talking about online, such as teeth whitening, bad breath, and braces. Sharing helpful information not only positions Colgate as caring about your needs and wants, not just their toothpaste sales, but also that Colgate is an authority above its competitors.

The bottom line? The next time you're in the market for toothpaste, Colgate hopes you will choose them.

Here's an example of how a local restaurant might *leverage* this distribution of content concept:

Blake Carver, a long-term friend and videographer (www.linke-din.com/in/blakecarvercreative), shot a short, punchy video for the Steer Inn, a local steak house in Orange County, CA. Imagine if they offered a free drink or dessert every time a patron shared that video on their Facebook wall while dining there? Imagine that happening 5 to 10 times per day! Potentially, tens of thousands of people would view that video for what would cost the restaurant only about one to two dollars per patron served.

"If you ask me what is the industry where content is the most important, it's 100 percent B2B. It's where content isn't just nice to have—it is 100 percent required." – Jay Baer

The Purpose of Branded Content

Branded Content is conducted for one sole purpose: to attract, acquire and engage a target audience so as to drive profitability. Even if you are running a non-profit, you will eventually need to recruit individual donors, volunteers and corporate supporters. But, as we saw in the Colgate example, your content should be much more editorial, educational and entertainment than sales-oriented.

The true power of Branded Content lies in the fact that people love a good story. So, tell your story like a story. **Power Brands** market content in a story format. And stories can be dramas, documentaries or even comedy. Your goal in storytelling is to present a captivating story that also directs your audience toward an intended response.

In his 2004 book, *The Seven Basic Plots: Why We Tell Stories*, Christopher Booker illuminates seven archetypal themes, which recur throughout every kind of storytelling.

1. **Overcoming the Monster.** Here the protagonist sets out to defeat an antagonistic force which threatens the protagonist, family or homeland. Examples: *War of the Worlds* and *The Magnificent Seven*

2. **Rags to Riches.** The poor protagonist acquires power, wealth, and a mate, loses it all and regains all upon growing as a person. Examples: *Cinderella, Aladdin,* and *David Copperfield.*

3. **The Quest.** The protagonist and some companions set out to acquire an important object or get to a location, facing many obstacles and temptations along the way. Examples: *The Wizard of Oz* and *The Lord of the Rings.*

4. **Voyage and Return.** The protagonist goes to a strange land and, after overcoming threats, returns with nothing but experience. Examples: *Alice in Wonderland* and *Gone with the Wind.*

5. **Comedy.** The protagonists are destined to be in love, but something keeps them apart, which is resolved by the end of the story. Examples: *Much Ado About Nothing* and *Four Weddings and a Funeral.*

6. **Tragedy.** The protagonist is a villain who falls from grace and whose death is a happy ending. Examples: *Macbeth* and *Bonnie and Clyde*

7. **Rebirth.** The protagonist is a villain or otherwise unlikable character who redeems him/herself over the course of the story. Examples: *Sleeping Beauty, Beauty and the Beast,* and *A Christmas Carol.*

While not all of these seven types of stories will apply to your specific business, one thing, for sure, is this: we all love a great story.

Storytelling is one of the most effective methods to invigorate your brand and connect with audiences. In fact, a great story is a primary component of a Branded Content campaign.

By giving your products and services life and relevancy, by capturing and sharing the stories that they really are, you can engage your target audience with a journey and/or experience they seek to enjoy.

In order for consumers to develop a deep, personal connection with your brand, your company stories must be genuine, creative and motivating.

"Brand storytelling isn't a new concept, but with the explosive growth of social media and content marketing, the opportunities to tell stories as part of direct and indirect brand marketing initiatives have become a strategic priority." – Forbes (Feb 2013)

Power Brands ignite and stoke the embers of interest by telling interesting stories. And great stories request and allow their audiences to help throw fuel on the fire.

Think about what gave rise to your brand, what inspired you to create your brand, as well as what your personal mission is to serve your community. Most importantly, clearly conceive in your mind what are the needs and values of your audience. Your brand's story must be compelling, genuine and creative. While it is important to tell your own story, customer narratives have the largest long-term impact on brands. The customer ought to be your main character, with your brand serving a *supporting role*, offering tools and opportunities that help your audience create success and satisfaction within their lives.

For example, if you're launching a marketing campaign for life insurance, your Branded Content should portray a story that focuses on how your customers have found peace of mind, because their family's financial security is now assured. Concentrate on one or two recipients, illustrating what your insurance plans represents to their family's security. Praise should always come from satisfied clients, in the form of a customer quote, not from a company spokesperson.

Testimonials will be your most powerful branding weapon to build legitimacy and customer loyalty. A testimonial that is just a few sentences is not memorable. A story that highlights a customer's personal life and challenges, chronicles the lengths an employee went to solve the problem, which illustrates a positive outcome, creates impact and will stick in readers' minds long after they move on from your marketing materials.

BECOMING A PUBLISHER OF BRANDED CONTENT

This may seem an odd concept, that you must become a publisher, but it may be one of the most significant changes that your brand could instigate in which to create a positive impact.

Remember my personal teenage story? Years ago, I created fliers, self-printed them and handed them out to local businesses. But this is not where people look these days. People used to read newspapers and look in the Yellow Pages book. Not any longer. People are looking online with their mobile devices!

A *Power Brand* must have an active presence on multiple media and must provide a wide selection of digital content that not only informs, educates, inspires, motivates and entertains, but also elevates and promotes new ideas every day to billions of people. That's where you need to be right now. As time rolls forward, your competitors are going to figure this out and begin acting like publishers and sharing their stories, keen insights and engaging information. You either need to hire professionals to do this for you, have it created in-house, or do a mixture of both.

In Rebecca Lieb's book, *Content Marketing: Think Like a Publisher – How to Use Content to Market Online and in Social Media,* she captures the key concept: **"Think like a publisher."**

So, what does a publisher think about? What does a publisher do?

YOUR EMPLOYEES CREATING CONTENT

"In five years the credibility of regular employees has increased dramatically ahead of that of the CEO. Since 2009, the credibility of regular employees has increased a full 20 percent more than any other category while trust in 'a person like yourself' has risen 15percent." – 2014 Elderman Trust Barometer

Many brands are recognizing that there best, most trusted sources for published content are the people who work for the brand. It requires strategic planning to ensure that your employees have access to market research, as well as how to stay aligned with your brand's message, so that they can become a powerful source of generating trust.

Employees not only have their unique perspective with the brand's day-to-day operations, but also possess a vast amount of technical expertise which they can share with your audiences.

PUBLISHING IS BRANDING

Publishing as a form of marketing seems counterintuitive to some business professionals, a distraction to where the focus should be: sales. But let me ask you this, would *you* rather be "sold," or presented with relevant and helpful information? Do you search the internet to be sold or are you seeking helpful or insightful information that is important and relevant to you? In today's marketplace, you have to take that consumer's point of view into deliberate consideration of how you want to be found, perceived and valued by targeted audiences.

I often tell my audiences and clientele that they should *not* build a website. Instead, they need to become a publisher and build their own ***Online Media Center.***

Do I mean that you should not build any website at all? No, what I mean is to not build a traditional website that sits there somewhat static, offering very little content and hoping to be found.

I strongly urge you to elevate your online game and convert your website presence to that of a media center. Just like a newspaper, publish articles. Just like a televised news channel, feature stories on video. Just like a publicist, distribute news through press releases and tweets. And just like a radio station, create podcasts.

Most websites today reflect the antiquated world of Don Draper of the famed television show *Mad Men*. Draper's world is replete with catch-phrases that promote outwards – *push* marketing – and attempts to persuade until people purchase. While content marketing is also ultimately held accountable for increasing revenues (ROI), how we go about it in today's world of "permission marketing" demands that we elevate our websites into online-media-center status.

Think of it this way: You are starting a newspaper, television station, PR firm and a radio station all rolled into one. Online marketing succeeds in today's world when you adopt the mindset of a publisher, not Don Draper's advertising era.

Publishers invite curiosity, exploration and thinking with information that is valuable, insightful or entertaining to us. Advertisers tended to overwhelm us with a message, trying to persuade us to buy and to buy again, no questions asked.

Advertising is an annoying, one-way communication channel. Public relations and effective content marketing is a two-way, interactive channel; just as Life itself is a two-way communication highway.

But when you examine websites or marketing efforts by major brands and small businesses, most are still not two-way or content-centric. They still mimic the ego-drunk, smoky haze of the outdated, Don Draper model.

But, hey! That's good for you! That gives you an opportunity before your competitors catch on!

The key to success today is to change one's thinking and strategy, to establish with clarity how we want to communicate our brand to encourage and engage people in a ***two-way discussion***. How do we want our brand received and perceived? From the onset, your content marketing strategy must be built upon a two-way communication model that is parallel to the laws of Life itself.

Elevate your online marketing planning and become an effective publisher with ***Power Brand*** content that includes:

* A comprehensive, written marketing strategy and step-by-step program for your online media center and your content management. How will your brand stand out?
* Conduct market research and content curation as a regular activity. There are simple methods on how to do this, covered later in this book.

- Blogging as a regular activity. One time a week is a minimum for solopreneurs and micro businesses. Larger, more established brands should ideally be posting 3-5 times a week.

- Blogs, posts and tweets that include leveraged "Newsjacking" (Covered later in the book.) to increase SEO value, as well as your relevance within your field.

- Guest blogging as a key part of your content strategy. Allowing guest bloggers to write for your site is a great way to mix up the views, as well as having those writers share their content from your site to their social media followers. Do the same by having your brand featured as guest-blog posts on others' sites.

- Regularly shared content across multiple social media channels. Your content can be repurposed in so many ways with social media.

- Social media fully utilized to engage with your audience by featured links to your site, making free offers and conducting surveys.

- White papers, eBooks and other "freemiums" distributed from your online media center. This is a great way to capture email addresses and offer high value to your followers and visitors.

- Automated marketing that follows up and nurtures your inquiries into sales or membership areas offering more content.

- Liberally utilized video content discoverable by key search terms. Video is fantastic for featuring successes, document case studies, and offered insight into your company and its products/services.

- Email treated like your daily or weekly newspaper. You should send on a regular basis emails with branded communications, such as newsletters, webinars and product offers, informing your audience of your best content.

- A dedicated page called "Media Room," or a page titled, "Media." Feature any and all positive press coverage, as well as key company information and contact data.
- Press releases intelligently used. Press releases can be abused as a method to build links. Google treats this as spam, so I suggest you conduct your press-release strategy prudently.
- Reviews on Yelp and Google My Business encouraged and managed. Respond to all reviews and address any unhappy clientele in a civil manner. *Online reviews are the most trusted content that people find online.*

BUILDING LOYALTY THROUGH BRANDED CONTENT

Consumer loyalty is no longer built on that Don Draper model, as consumers realize they have so many more choices. Consumers also possess access to a vast amount of third-party reviews to judge you before committing to a purchase.

83 percent of consumers say that online reviews influence their perceptions about companies and eight out of 10 American internet users say that negative information they read online made them change their mind about a purchase decision. And, yes, online reviews can be considered Branded Content. What better spokesperson could there ever be than satisfied customers touting their story about your company?

Brands that listen and create content that fills voids and elevates our minds and lives will build trust and viable relationships; thus, brand loyalty.

Your vibe will attract your tribe.

Additionally, you will be providing your best customers with some great content that will compel them to share your message across their own channels, blogs and social media circles.

CHAPTER 13

Crowdsourcing Your
Branded Content

You ARE MOST LIKELY THINKING to yourself right now, "I get it. Branded content is important. But, where do I find time, human capital, resources and the inspiration to create this branded content?" Crowdsourcing your content offers a huge, potential solution. Crowdsourcing is:

> "A slang term used to describe the practice of using both the skills and time of underpaid — or unpaid — amateurs to create content or solutions for established businesses. Basically, crowdsourcing means to 'use talents of the crowd', and is a play on the word outsourcing. The origins of the word crowdsourcing are credited to *Jeff Howe*, a *Wired Magazine* writer." – Webopedia

> "Crowdsourcing is a method of solving problems through the distributed contributions of multiple people. It's used to address tough problems that happen every day. Ideas for new opportunities. Ways to solve problems. Uncovering an existing approach that addresses your need." – Hutch Carpenter (www.bhc3.com)

Crowdsourcing brings to mind fundraising or crowdfunding, where several or many individuals pool together small amounts of money that add up to meeting an overall financial goal. In the content marketing world, a similar benefit can be garnered with crowdsourcing: innovation and resources.

Small businesses that crowdsource bright ideas through online interactions can tap into unlimited talent pools of geniuses. With intelligent crowdsourcing, their content initiatives can generate amazing amounts of excellent content quickly, efficiently and affordably.

If you are seeking feedback on your customer service or types of additional products or services to potentially offer, who better to ask than the people those changes will affect most? Who better to involve in the messaging of your brand and brand benefits than those most passionately connected with your brand?

THE POWER OF CROWDSOURCING CONTENT

"The power of the crowd is the ability to draw from the collective memory, expertise and experience of many people at the same time," said Jessica Greenwalt, founding member and lead designer of the crowdsourced medical-diagnosis platform, CrowdMed.

Without a doubt, crowdsourcing with your audience leverages the collective insight and genius of your existing audience. Here are your eyes and ears, your "boots on the ground" that can provide real-time intel and content. Crowdsourcing is accurate and rapid, survey-data collection, as well as a resource for creative content.

"If you want people to be emotionally connected to and invested in your business, everyone has to think they matter as a customer," said Jon Olinto, co-founder of the b.good Family Foundation, which puts its annual grant recipient up to a consumer vote. "As long as you're willing to turn some decisions over to the customers, you can empower them. Anyone who participates is automatically engaged with the company and part of its story."

To a certain degree, most every business uses crowdsourcing already, although they may not view it as such. But believe me, they rely on it heavily. Case in point: customer reviews are crowdsourcing collaborations. Reviews on Yelp, Angie's List, Google My Business and other sites are considered valuable content by consumers. So, if this is occurring naturally, should you not consider taking control of this phenomenon and become proactive with it? Yes, you should.

Crowdsourced content can include:

* Customer reviews
* Guest blog posts
* Success stories and testimonials
* Case studies
* Check-ins on social media
* Videos mentioning your brand or its benefits
* Press coverage, media mentions, or peer-to-peer journal articles

HELPFUL CROWDSOURCING TIPS

If you're thinking about integrating crowdsourcing into your marketing strategy, here are a few helpful tips:

* **Build a community and showcase your core purpose.** Nothing generates more crowdsourced content than people participating with a brand that shows genuine compassion and purpose. Communities built around core-value activities and a great purpose, with notable and worthwhile results to show off, will find people wanting to contribute to them on so many levels, content being just one of them.

- **Allow creativity to blossom.** Customers appreciate creative content crowdsourced by other consumers, than "buy me now" promotional content. Allow creativity and fun to imbue your content. Invite it, nurture it, and celebrate it.

- **Engage with commenters.** Engaging with those who comment, favorably or otherwise, elicits key information and insight. Commenters and your exchange with them can not only provide you real-time, genuine intel, but also spark new ideas for future content. Interact with people and listen to their ideas and critiques.

- **Utilize surveys and polls.** Survey tools are available to help you reach out to your audience and get valuable feedback. Not only can you evaluate collected information to create better, more on-point content in the future, but the data can be repurposed into blog posts, video reports and Infographics.

- **Work with influencers.** Discover the top bloggers and social-media movers and shakers. Narrow down to who's generating the most relevant conversations in your industry or circles. Establish contact with those influencers by following them online or posting comments to some of their content. You can create important relationships by first making them aware that you exist. It is important that you inform the influencer of your value proposition to them. You accomplish this by creating content about them from your site. This exposure to a broader audience demonstrates your willingness to assist them in reaching a broader audience. Find their "go button," get their agreement, and then leverage their name. Thus, you gain access to broader audiences.

- **Use social media to ask people what they want.** Social media is a perfect channel to find those who will engage with your content. It is key to have great titles and a strong call to action within your post or tweet. If you want content or feedback, you need to ask for it. Sharing your blog posts and videos across your social media is an obvious action. Not so obvious is reading and interacting with the comments. Ask or invite your audience to help you create content: "Tell us how our _____ has helped you to _____better" can be a winner. Customer-generated content has the greatest potential to go viral, becoming your best content.

* **Ask your followers to create products or services**. This can be done directly or as a contest. Asking your followers and customers what they would like to see you offer or sell, discovers hidden or emerging needs. Kodak should have done this about 15 years ago; they might have stopped making film and jumped early and fast into digital photography and software.
* **Create clear-cut boundaries.** Control the social and public conversation as best as possible. Never let your content and message get hijacked by others trying to ride your coat tails of promotion, or make you look like a fool.

As you sit back and contemplate your content-marketing strategy, never forget to engage with your community and to solicit their input. Every industry and niche community is different. Each offers its own quality insight and creative innovation. *Power Brands* accomplish their objectives by using crowdsourcing as a tactic to grow their social networks and elevate their followers to become active brand advocates for them.

How to Overcome "Writers' Block" In Creating Branded Content

The inspiration for your brand content... where does it come from, what kills it and how to do you revive it? Whether author, blogger, videographer, screenwriter, poet or songwriter, getting inspired to create content, at times, is difficult. Sooner or later, the wall referred to as "writers' block" will find most. I have covered this topic before on my personal blog (www.edwindearborn.com/blog), suggesting that people should get some space by riding a motorcycle at such times. But that limited the remedy to those willing to ride a motorcycle.

While I still "get out and ride" as a form of workable therapy, the majority of my fellow content-creators can take a stroll outside, hike a trail, or ride a bicycle to get some free space.

My other tip is this: "crowdsource" your inspiration by consuming the content of others.

MY DIRTY LITTLE SECRET

A dirty little secret crept up on me; it caught me by surprise until I realized how addicted I had become to this new method for insight and inspiration.

Writing this book, I needed to conduct quite a bit of research. Actually, more than just a bit. These days the typical and easiest research resource for any content creator is Google. So, while writing, I took full advantage of this resource, following my own catch-phrase, "Don't be frugal with the Google." But, honestly, I could only take so much screen-staring and endless reading of streams of text. To my great relief, as you will also discover, I found out that Google quite often offers up online videos, not just links to text. Therein lies my dirty little secret, as massive inspiration to overcome a huge barrier for me and most content creators.

You see, standard video marketing protocol is to create pithy, but entertaining, informative, short videos. Even Vine has cut down video messages to six seconds, with massive success.

According to research conducted by the Jun Group (2011), videos that are 15 seconds or less are shared 37 percent more often than those between 30 seconds and one minute. Video longer than a minute? That sharing stat goes *down to* shared only 18 percent more often than videos of longer than one minute.

According to research by Visible Measures, 20 percent of your viewers will click away from a video in 10 seconds or less. It doesn't get a lot better after that. You'll lose about 1/3 of your viewers by 30 seconds, 45 percent by one minute, and almost 60 percent by two minutes. And those numbers remain the same *no matter how long the length of the video.*

Longer video is where the inspiration to create content exists! Have you ever looked at a video on YouTube or Vimeo indicating that it was 30, 60 or even 80 minutes long, telling yourself, "No way am I watching that one"? Commitment to watching and getting into the nitty-gritty and the audience Q&A of a long video was something that was not only a barrier for me, but apparently for many others as well, based on the aforementioned stats. When looking at how many views these longer videos had, their stats were much, much lower than their shorter counterparts.

And that's my dirty little secret!

The longer videos contain the most intriguing ideas and discussions that can spark your own "Aha moments," offering up new insights and the very fodder of inspiration that you need to help you climb over the writers' block preventing your creative content ideation.

MY SIMPLE, YET HIGHLY EFFECTIVE PROTOCOL

This outlines how I become inspired and begin creating my own content, step-by-step:

1. Determine the subject matter or exact topic for which you want insight. Grab a notepad and a pen, or whatever you use

to keep notes. (I'm old school and still like writing on a yellow pad.)

2. Go to YouTube and type into their search bar your subject, being as specific as possible. For instance, if I was interested in "branding," I would narrow my search down to "small business branding," as this was more my target audience for my upcoming book.

3. Look for authorities in the field and narrow down to which video you want to watch. Then watch that long video.

4. Keep notes of all your ideas, small and large, that are sparked. (Often, I will stop the video momentarily while I make my notes.)

5. Let the flow of ideation occur and take breaks, when needed, to complete your thoughts. If you need to walk around, have a cigarette or a coffee or grab a bite to eat, this is completely acceptable. The point is to learn to spark the inspiration for your content, or small segments of content, by working within a greater body of work.

THE CONTENT MYTH

False expectations in business, branding, marketing, and in daily life always lead to unnecessary disappointment. The idea that all of your content or crowdsourced content is going to go viral, or that in some way you can jerry-rig your content to manipulate audience desires and force your content to go viral, is wishful thinking.

That people are going to bang down your doors the minute you tweet something, email it, post it on your blog or YouTube, is delusionary. Anyone claiming to know how they can make your content go viral is a sure sign that you should not conduct business with them.

The few, isolated examples of viral magic that have occurred do inspire us all and make us dream big, but these are so far from the norm, even for **Power Brands**. There simply is no secret code or insider's bag of tricks that will make your content go viral or create massive demand in a matter of days or weeks.

The actual pathway to content success is to understand deeply what people need and want — what solves the problems they perceive — and then create the content, products and services that consistently meet or exceed their expectations in those areas.

Rather than try to crack the code on how to make your content "viral-prone," I recommend that you develop a branding and marketing strategy that can be consistently implemented. I would be thinking how to create content that genuinely resonates among my audience, and which has traction for those seeking what I have to offer.

Over time, after you have reached and touched hearts and minds, those people will come to love and trust your brand, your work-ethic, services and products. Additionally, they will feel inspired to share them with others.

The real secret to brand success is not creating viral content, but creating content that:

1. Connects to your ever-growing AUDIENCE,
2. Is on-target with your core MESSAGE,
3. Is published with FREQUENCY, and
4. Creates genuine conversation around ENGAGEMENT.

CHAPTER 14

Supporting Your Branding with Infrastructure

WITHOUT A SOUND INFRASTRUCTURE YOUR branding efforts will fall short and will not gain traction with key players in the online world. Organizations which are badly organized will not develop and distribute high-quality content on a consistent basis, nor will they render to-notch, rapid service to their customers.

Lack of infrastructure can implode the Branding Triangle regardless of how sexy and well-designed the Brand Image may be. Lack of infrastructure will waste the majority of your branding-marketing expenditures.

What do I mean by infrastructure?

Infrastructure is having in place the strategy, policies, team members (employees or outsourced help), business processes, organizational patterns, training and know-how to ensure that you communicate your unique position in the marketplace and the benefits you bring to the lives of others.

"Infrastructure refers to the basic physical and organizational structures needed for the operation of a society or enterprise, or the services and facilities necessary for an economy to function." – Wikipedia

What are your brand's "basic physical and organizational structure" and necessary "services and facilities" so that it can function and be economically sound?

I've posed the questions here, what are your answers? Write them down.

Without a sound understanding of the importance of an infrastructure for your brand in terms of functionality, your business could fail without you ever really knowing why. Every brand, to succeed must have support services, effective personnel, staff training, and other organizational logistics in place and operational. Like a bridge spanning a wide chasm, your brand must be built upon strong pillars or support beams.

Here is a minimum-basics checklist of what your branding infrastructure should contain. Copy it and add to and adapt this list to your own needs.

Brand infrastructure list:

- Sound consumer research
- Keyword research
- Mission statement, well publicized
- A written, strategic brand strategy
- A contextual content strategy
- Social media and content policies
- Well-developed marketing and PR budget
- Marketing and Sales KPI's (A performance indicator or Key Performance Indicator (**KPI**) is a type of performance measurement.) and quotas
- Corporate ethics policy
- A unique selling proposition (USP)
- Distinctive logo, colors and packaging

- Uniforms or dress code
- Company training manuals & courses
- Customer support staff
- Company website and blog
- Appropriate, branded, social channels
- An organizational chart
- A CMO, Director of Marketing or someone similar
- Marketing staff (designers, writers, bloggers, videographers, Audio/Visual people, etc.)
- Strong relations with KOL's (Key Opinion Leaders), marketing partners, strategic relationships and affiliates
- Internal communications system and schedules
- Schedules for events and activities
- Joint venture relationships with other brands

Branding is much more successful, sustainable and profitable when supported by a well-built and tightly organized infrastructure and team.

BRANDING AND MARKETING IS NOT AN "EXPENSE"

The false idea that literally cripples more small businesses and their owners is that marketing is an "expense." Marketing budgets, marketing and strategy planning, and logistics are a part of that *infrastructure;* as such, these are vital for forward progress. By analogy, the equation is simple: marketing is the engine that drives sales, and finance is the required fuel that powers your branding and marketing engine. Your marketing budget is the fuel line.

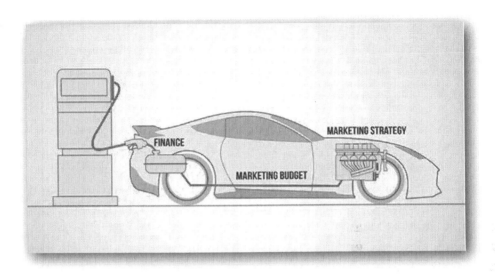

I do not doubt that a few CPAs will argue my statement, pointing to ledgers and complicated textbooks from fancy universities to attempt to prove me wrong. But mine is a pragmatic truth.

The argument begs the question: What, really, is a budget?

"A budget is a quantitative expression of a plan for a defined period of time. It may include planned sales volumes and revenues, resource quantities, costs and expenses, assets, liabilities and cash flows. It expresses strategic plans of business units, organizations, activities or events in measurable terms." – Wikipedia

Not using the word "budget" from an accountant's perspective, my sense speaks to the mind-set and strategic planning of a successful entrepreneur.

Have you ever heard of a major startup or a new invention originated by a CPA or a bookkeeper? Very rarely. Business geniuses and marketing mavericks rarely get an OK from a committee or a CPA before launching their idea to the world. They may consult these types along the way, but their courage to launch comes from deep inside of them, not from corporate accounts ledgers. Trust me, most CPAs will readily admit that their industry dwells in last place when it comes to marketing innovation and branding prowess.

MARKETING CREATES DESIRE (REACH)

The essence of marketing activity is the creation of desire and exchange – moving products and/or services into the hands of consumers directly and through Sales personnel. Manufacturing and Accounting cannot achieve that end-product. Accounting surely cannot achieve that on their own; nor do Boards of Directors and their annual meetings. Only intelligent branding and marketing can create desire and move massive amounts of product or services into the hands of eager buyers, directly or through sales staffs.

To pigeonhole and devalue the role of branding and marketing as an "expense" opens the door for failure. Agreeing with that *false notion,* too many business locomotives that might have been successes have stopped cold in their tracks before ever getting out of the station.

All small business marketing strategies that would move the business forward and upward require:

1. A comprehensive strategy to drive it.
2. An adequate budget to fuel it.

I often tell my clients, "I manage two of the most important elements in branding and marketing: strategies and budgets."

When General Eisenhower landed in France for the D-Day invasion, did he have a strategy before he attacked? Most certainly. Were his armed forces supported by logistics, infrastructure and a budget? You bet! He had a blank check from Congress and millions of Americans at home buying war bonds and building armaments. Eisenhower's strategic military success was built upon a strategy well supported by an infrastructure and a budget.

Unfortunate it is that too many business people cut their marketing budgets in a knee-jerk reaction when they encounter financial strain, cutting back on marketing efforts is the last thing that should be done when times are tough.

Intelligent promotion, effectively executed, is the best path out of financial stress. Research has proven time and again conclusively: those companies that increase marketing budgets and strategic initiatives during hard times expand far in excess of their competitors once the economy makes an upswing.

This is too easy to prove: business parks, malls and small businesses that are empty of clientele, are a dime a dozen; and yet their shelves are full with unsold merchandise.

The key with small-business marketing is to be proactive and consistent. Let me reiterate these two crucial points again as this not idle advice. Being proactive is the opposite of worrying and blaming the economy or your competition. Lack of consistency forces 90 percent of small business marketing efforts to fail.

"My main contention is that at the heart all business failures are actually marketing failures. Marketing is really a philosophy and there's a lot of good companies that are really good at marketing but don't have a marketing department. They have an external orientation so they look at what's going on outside and force themselves to ask uncomfortable questions about what external trends they need in their business." - Martin Glenn, CEO of United Biscuits and former Pepsico marketer

Marketing is vital and an integral part of the planning for any business's success and profitability. When marketing lowers in status to a mere "expense", and thus is cut, a business diminishes its chances for continued success and growth.

How to Develop a Functional Marketing Budget

A functional marketing budget will fuel continual growth for any small business. Unfortunately, in a world dominated by accounting principles and executives untrained in marketing, marketing budgets appear to be inapplicable business tools to most startups, entrepreneurs and small business owners.

The problem begins when one starts a business and does not realize *the estimation of effort* required to launch, market and sustain a small business or start-up into the marketplace. Most small business owners so wrap themselves up in taking care of their customers that they rarely carve out any time to breath, let alone properly plan, brand and market their small business.

Within the first few years of operation, one should allocate a heavy amount of the budget to marketing, as much as one can possibly afford. I suggest 10% of your gross as a minimum.

Of course, your marketing budget and the amount allocated to it is going to depend on the type of business that you are operating, as well as your profit margin. If you are in an industry where profit margins are considerable, you should be spending a higher amount on marketing to ensure that your business garners as much attention and public interest as possible.

When coming up with an annual figure for marketing costs, don't forget about related expenses, which can include market research, attending trade shows, training yourself and others, and hiring experts to help you with special projects, such as improving your website and creating engaging content.

Several years ago, *Inc. Magazine* surveyed 500 of the fastest-growing private companies in America. Those companies' chief executives were asked to estimate their sales and marketing expenses as a percentage of overall revenues. The average? Almost 11 percent, with several close to the 20 percent range. Now, with a more competitive marketplace since that survey was conducted, one needs to match this percentage level or spend an even higher budgetary amount to ensure that the *correct* branding message arrives and creates the desired impact on the bottom line.

HOW MARKETING BUDGETS HAVE BEEN
TRADITIONALLY ESTABLISHED

When most small businesses and entrepreneurs establish a marketing budget, the predominant, traditionally employed principle creates a non-competitive edge. The typical standard is, "What is my industry standard?" The problem with that standard is twofold:

1. Do we know that this "standard" is effective?
2. Does this amount align with the proper estimation of effort required to meet our revenue objectives in the current environment?

Setting your budget to an accepted "industry standard" will not give you a competitive edge. To achieve one's sales objective is really just a question of reverse engineering. In other words, we must work backwards from establishing the sales objectives; then continue to work backwards to the strategic plan; and then to the accompanying budget and tactics that will meet those objectives.

The real question that you should be asking yourself is, "What are my sales goals that I am absolutely committed to achieving?" Once determined, *that* benchmark sets the standard for the activities that will set the margins of the marketing budget.

The most common method of reverse engineering is to ask the small business owner how much revenue he or she would like to generate per month or for the year. Based on those numbers, we can compare that goal to how much revenue the small business is already achieving.

For example, if the business owner wanted to expand their monthly revenue from $50,000 per month to $100,000 per month, we would have to minimally double the marketing efforts and budget. More likely, though, we would have to triple the efforts and budget to ensure an *abundance* of revenue-generating opportunities and activity. By correctly assessing the estimation of effort, we could establish a marketing budget that will support the plan and goals.

MARKETING BUDGETS & THE MARKETING PLAN

Possession of a proper marketing budget is only the beginning of the process. Remember, your marketing plan is the engine that drives the sales and consumption of your products or services, while the marketing budget fuels that engine. Both are vitally important, forming a symbiotic relationship.

To pump new revenue into any business requires a comprehensive marketing plan that is fueled by a marketing budget. As the business grows, that engine can become more complex and more fuel can be added. When a marketing plan and marketing budget are managed in such a light, the whole process can take on a new meaning and significance toward the growth of any small business.

YOUR MARKETING BUDGET DURING RECESSIONS AND TOUGH TIMES

A McGraw-Hill research study of over 600 businesses showed that during the early 1980's recession, businesses that increased their ad spending had, by 1985, witnessed a 256% growth in sales over companies that had cut back on advertising.

The opposite is true as well. In 2002, a year of economic expansion, 80% of the businesses that increased their marketing budgets had no gain in market share.

This is because everybody increases their marketing budgets during economic expansion. In other words, keeping a steady marketing budget when others cut down is a short-term struggle with a long-term benefit.

While the above statistics are counter-intuitive to how we traditionally manage a budget, it is important to note that our best opportunity exists when other brands are pulling back and hunkering down for the storm. This is the exact time where *Power Brands* seize opportunity as their competitors begin to abandon their marketing initiatives.

"When economic hard times loom, we tend to retreat to our village. Look for cozy hearth-and-home family scenes in advertising to replace images of extreme sports, adventure and rugged individualism. Zany humor and appeals on the basis of fear are out." - Harvard Business Review

CHAPTER 15

Why Strategy is So Important

WHEN I WRITE ABOUT STRATEGY, my message is not reserved for big, established brands, for often it is the small business leaders who say, "We have no time for strategy because..." believing this is a futile and inapplicable exercise.

Strategy - "A plan of action or policy designed to achieve a major or overall aim." [Greek *stratēgein* 'be a general', from *stratēgos*, from *stratos* 'army' + *agein* 'to lead.']

Coaching a business on their marketing challenges and opportunities, my first action is to ask a question, "May I see a copy of your ***written*, strategic marketing plan?" leaving 98 percent of them embarrassed.

As you may have guessed, they could not produce a written plan because they did not have one.

HEAR THIS:

YOUR BRAND'S INHERIT BRILLIANCE WILL NOT ASSURE ITS SUCCESS. HOW WELL YOU EXECUTE *WRITTEN*, STRATEGIC PLANS AND TACTICS IS YOUR BEST ASSURANCE OF SUCCESS.

DISCIPLINE + BRILLIANCE IS *THE* IDEAL *POWER BRAND* SCENARIO.

Imagine a general leading an army into battle without a strategy. It's easy to see that he would not only lose the battle, but also men would die needlessly in a failed attempt. History's grandest empires have disappeared because of omitted written, incompetent, or conflicting strategic planning.

Strategic planning is the primary stage for success in military operations, sports, business, and branding and marketing. While your "soldiers" won't die on the business battlefield, your losses will be a lot of money and trusted contacts, if you enter business skirmishes in a hit-or-miss manner rather than an analytical, strategic path.

Strategy does not concern itself with the "next step." Strategy concerns itself with multiple, pre-planned and sequential steps, always with the overall goal in mind.

Before you expend money and effort with branding and marketing you need to sit down and write out a comprehensive strategy for your business, which would, of course, include your marketing and sales tactics. Your strategy should be as broad, and your tactics as specific, as possible...

* Who does what action, when?
* What target audiences do you want to reach and convert?
* What type of market research will you conduct?
* When will certain objectives need to be reached and by what date?
* What are the objectives (goals)?
* Who will pay for the actions... how and when?
* How will performance be measured?

If you are worried that you do not know how to draft such a plan, let me give you some helpful tips. There are plenty of resources, free and paid, to help you build a solid strategy. Do not worry about building the "perfect plan." Write out a strategy that helps you gain clarity and a sense of direction, as well as permit you to see what resources you have to leverage. Also list the challenges you foresee that you will have to overcome as you move forward.

Here are more resources you can access to help you craft and write your brand-marketing strategy:

- Locate a business contact who has created such a plan, and see if he or she will mentor you through the process.
- Check with your social media contacts. Maybe someone you know would be willing to help you for free, or for a reasonable fee.
- Don't be frugal with Google. Search and find free or inexpensive templates that can guide you through your marketing plan.
- YouTube is a wonderful resource. I am consistently amazed at how much helpful content exists on YouTube. (When I typed, *"how to write a marketing strategy"* in YouTube's search bar, there were 55,000 results.)
- Check with your local SBA for sponsored workshops covering a myriad of topics, including planning, branding and marketing.

ANCIENT TREATISE ON STRATEGY

One of the most famous and oft-quoted works on strategy is Chinese general Sun Tzu's *The Art of War,* commonly regarded as the definitive work on military strategy and tactics. Written over 2,500 years ago, *The Art of War* has remained the most important military treatise in Asia, and has influenced Eastern and Western military thinking, business strategic, tactical and legal planning.

Making the case for planned strategy are the eloquent words of Sun Tzu: "Victorious warriors win first and then go to war, while defeated warriors go to war first and then seek to win."

According to the Department of Trade and Industry, up to one fifth of 400,000 annual business startups fail within the first 12 months of operation. This gives us an approximate figure of 80,000 businesses failing annually, which is over 10,000 per week!

According to the SBA, 50 percent of small businesses fail in their first five years.

Do you believe that all these businesses developed, followed and regularly reviewed their strategic business plans, or marketing plans? From my experience as a business coach and brand strategist, that would be a resounding "No!"

"Customer-centric and competitively dominant marketing strategies are vital to business success." - Harvard Business Review

In business, strategic planning is the mind that directs and moves the body. A body without a sentient mind is a *zombie*. Brands walking around like zombies never think analytically or act intelligently.

TACTICS WITHOUT STRATEGY

Consider the antithesis. Imagine only tactics without strategy. Imagine daily, weekly and quarterly tactics implemented with zero reference to an overall strategy and goal. Imagine a brand that simply shows up and takes whatever action needed to **react** to what happens that day or week. That would be like trying to play only defense in football, expecting to score enough points to win.

Engaging solely with defensive marketing is reactionary. Classic examples would be handling referrals whenever they happen to walk in of their own accord, or responding to negative online reviews once they have appeared.

Analytical business branding and marketing is primarily offensive, not defensive. This is by predetermined choice. Analytically based branding figures out how to maximize generating more referrals and reviews with proactive initiatives and programs.

Power Brand strategic planning is about how to perform on both sides of the offense/defense paradigm with a heavier emphasis on offense intending to score more "marketing points."

Unfortunately, those who think only in the here-and-now mentally block out thinking and planning for the future. We live in an instant-gratification society, which has become accustomed to failure and waste. Too many companies and individuals are caught up with blaming the economy, Congress, or their DNA for their losses. When you have a "reason" to, it's easy to justify failure.

What sets great ***Power Brands*** (and their marketing strategies) apart is the time devoted to developing and enforcing a well-crafted, written strategic plan founded on sound market research.

THE FOUNDATION OF STRATEGY IS MARKET RESEARCH

In military circles, planning gathers critical data on the enemy and terrain as intelligence ("intel"). In business, planning refers to this function as Market Research.

Research - "The systematic investigation into and study of materials and sources in order to establish facts and reach new conclusions." [From Old French *re-* (expressing intensive force) + *cerchier* 'to search.']

Branding and marketing - to be successful - must be based on market research. Research determines who is your right audience or audiences, and discovers what they truly need and want. Something that they want more than not; a cause they deem worth supporting; a problem they want solved; or a great opportunity they would love to take advantage of — these are the goals of Research.

Your research includes finding out what to say, how to say it, content-wise, and on which media channels that message should be delivered. What types of branded content are currently consumed, and what will be consumed? What are the favored social media channels to use? Well, you get the idea.

Generals who send armies into battle with no or faulty intelligence do not last long. Neither do business executives.

Here are the antonyms of *intelligence* in the English dictionary: ignorance, stupidity, inability and ineptness. Hero or Zero — what's your choice?

TOO BUSY FOR RESEARCH

"Research" sounds ominous to most startups, entrepreneurs and small business professionals strapped for time or the finances to conduct research correctly. Their idea of research connotes *expensive, complex, time-consuming*; therefore, "Not for me." Maybe in the past that was somewhat plausible, but today, great research is easily and rapidly obtained, and much more affordable.

THE ORIGINAL MAD MAN

Learning and knowing the writings of David Ogilvy is a giant step toward being a success in marketing. Ogilvy is the model on which the long-running TV show *Mad Men* was inspired and built. In fact, the BBC aired a program on David Ogilvy titled *The Original Mad Man*. Mr. Ogilvy has also been referred to as the "Father of Modern Advertising."

David Ogilvy was born in 1911. He grew up in poverty in Scotland. His father was a failed businessman; his mother ambitious, eccentric and highly intelligent. Both parents influenced him. From his father's failure he inherited an insatiable desire for success. His positive mental acuity came from his mother.

In 1938, Ogilvy went to America to work for Gallup Research. There he cut his teeth on the importance and techniques of Market Research.

Ogilvy never stopped thinking, "What does the consumer think?" To this day the Advertising Research Foundation (ARF) David Ogilvy Award celebrates market research and its ability to guide the creation of advertising that taps into consumer needs and desires, a reminder that market research plays a pivotal role in our consumer lives.

Ogilvy developed research at Gallup that could foretell the success of a film according to a number of factors, including the movie stars. He and his cronies witnessed first-hand the predictive power of well-conducted market research. Unfortunately, the movie stars felt threatened by his findings and pushed Ogilvy out of Hollywood. In response, Ogilvy stuck to his guns and founded his own ad agency, further influencing Hollywood and the American society in more ways than anyone had envisioned at the time. Ogilvy's "intellectual honesty" of market research remains today more relevant than most modern writings on the subject.

Imagine if your market research was based on the factor of "intellectual honesty." Great qualities for any brand in a world of content marketing, online reviews and transparency.

My Three Favorite and Proven Research Methods

There are more options in market research today than in Ogilvy's time. Market Research is quite an extensive subject, covering vast amounts of technologies, techniques and information. True market researchers have studied many thousands of hours and they do comprehend their craft with great expertise. To the SMB professional these vast resources are inaccessible most in terms of time and expense, but ***Power Branding Secrets*** intends to unlock the inaccessibility of branding and marketing for anyone wishing to excel in business. To that end, I believe that these three following research methods will help you build your ***Power Brand:***

1.) Survey your target audience. You can conduct this research through in-person surveys, emailed surveys, and by reading surveys that others have conducted on similar audiences. Such surveys are available online and through industry publications.

2.) Reverse engineer — break down something to see how it works — the success of other businesses similar to your own. This yields valid survey data about how another brand successfully conducts business and what is working. For instance, if I wanted to open an independent café, I would interview the top 10 café owners and compile a list of their most successful actions and replicate those actions exactly in my business venture. By careful study of success in a related business one can emulate it and just as methodically incorporate those actions into one's business.

3.) Social media used as a research tool can give you incredible insight. Since social media continues every second of every day globally, you can leverage social media by taking its pulse of what is being talked about and by whom directly. One way would be to look at the social channels *of your competitors*. View their Twitter feeds, Amazon and Yelp reviews; YouTube videos and blog posts and see what is resonating. What type of feedback are they getting? What is being discussed as feedback, good or bad? What of theirs is being shared most? These *social signals* will give you insight to what is gaining traction and interest.

"There's too much talking in social media and not enough listening and learning. There's too much 'me' in social media and not enough 'we' in the social web." - Brian Solis

If you were to follow all three methods - surveys, reverse engineering and social media research - concurrently, can you imagine the insight that you would gain into your customer's mindset, as well as the insight and know-how garnered from those who have successfully overcome the challenges of your business and marketing model? Your chances of hitting a **Power Brand** home run would increase dramatically. Your brand's success potential would expand exponentially over competitors who took a shot in the dark with their gut feelings alone.

Insightful market research will be your backbone of marketing and business success. And that research is not a one-time action. You should have market research infrastructure in place as one of your ongoing business processes, collecting customer feedback and online reviews, and continuing to survey, survey, survey to spot consumer trends to take advantage of on a continual basis.

Lastly, and almost without writing it, you must know that listening to your customers to meet their needs and requests will make your brand and your branded content stand out, get noticed and get shared by those who know you have taken the time and effort to understand them.

SETTING GOALS AND OBJECTIVES FOR MARKETING STRATEGY

I had an intriguing conversation with a long-term friend of mine concerning how top corporations develop and implement strategic plans. During our discussion he asked me, "Do you know the difference between a goal and an objective?" I had to admit I had never pondered this important question prior to his asking.

Goals and objectives have become synonymous in the business world and this is creating a confusion that is evidenced by the lack of accomplishment and growth among too many brands. In many dictionaries the two words are referenced as synonyms so it is easy to see why there is a mix-up. But, there are important differences.

So, what is the difference between a goal and an objective?

Goal: "The object toward which an endeavor is directed; an end. A *goal* is something rewarding or fulfilling that inspires a sustained endeavor." - American Heritage Dictionary

Objective: "A specific result that a person or system aims to achieve within a time frame and with available resources. In general, objectives are more specific and easier to measure than goals. Objectives are basic tools that underlie all planning and strategic activities. They serve as the basis for creating policy and evaluating performance. Some examples of business objectives include minimizing expenses, expanding internationally, or making a profit." - BusinessDictionary.com

To reach your rewarding goal in business, you must remain inspired to achieve key objectives. You must do this with available resources and within a specified time frame. The two definitions are important enough to commit to memory as these concepts apply as much to branding as they do to any business.

One can have the goal of becoming a successful business owner or a published author. But as you may already know, there are many objectives that one must achieve before one enjoys the satisfaction of having reached the goal.

"Management by objective works - if you know the objectives. Ninety percent of the time you don't." - Peter Drucker

It can be clearly observed and stated that many individuals never attain their goals because they never set required objectives and then make those objectives occur, come hell or high water. *Power Brands* distinguish themselves by having definitive goals and articulated, specific, written objectives.

The end-game of achieved objectives and attained goals makes branding much more strategic than most people have realized.

POWER BRANDING IS ABOUT CONSISTENCY

As we have seen here, successful relationships are built on trust more than any other factor. *Trust is developed through consistency of message, values and actions.* People and company brands that are inconsistent with their communications, tone (attitude), values and predictable actions are not trusted and, therefore, rejected by the marketplace. It's been that way since the dawn of Man.

"Success is neither magical nor mysterious. Success is the natural consequence of consistently applying basic fundamentals." — Jim Rohn

Again, one of the most important elements of your branding is consistency.

Inconsistent customer service will not build trust or loyalty. Inconsistency with your social media marketing will not build followers, or generate likes, retweets or shares. **Inconsistency is a complete brand killer.**

The biggest sources of inconsistency are:

1. Lack of strategic planning.
2. Lazy management and no accountability.
3. Weak or no team building and training.

CONSISTENCY IS NOT OBNOXIOUS

One can swing toward the other side of the pendulum and be so "consistent" that your brand becomes annoying. Barraging your followers with daily emails and 80 tweets per day will not build trust and loyalty. This will burn bridges and besmudge and reposition your brand as something *undesirable* and not to be associated with in the future. An important element within your consistency is acceptability. Instead, study your audience well and determine what types of messages you will be sending through social channels and how often.

CHAPTER 16

When Branding, Marketing and Sales Come Together

ALL THIS BRANDING AND MARKETING planning, infrastructure and activity has a singular purpose: to increase customer acquisitions and sales.

Sell - *"Give or hand over (something) in exchange for money."* [Old Norse *selja* 'give up, sell'. Early use included the sense 'give, hand (something) over voluntarily in response to a request']

REPUTATIONS VERSUS EXPECTATIONS

Large and small businesses around the world struggle to connect the work of "marketing people" with "salespeople." In fact, Fournaise Marketing Group's (www.fournaisegroup.com) 2012 *Global Marketing Effectiveness Program*, wherein they interviewed more than 1,200 CEO's across North America, Europe, Asia and Australia, found that over 70 percent of CEO's do not expect their marketing teams to generate increased sales.

While the report confirms that the majority of those CEOs possess their own in-house marketing departments, they do so "purely out of tradition." Sadly, defeatism has permeated most CEO's. Per the same report, they made the "conscious decision not to expect more from marketing than branding."

Compounding the problem, widespread consensus is that marketing professionals live too much in a creative and social-media bubble. CEOs don't find their own marketing professionals to be return-on-investment (ROI) focused; i.e., intent on budget accountability, correlating directly with spent money and achieved objectives and goals, which make a positive impact on the Profit and Loss statement.

A mere 20 percent of CEO's contend that their top marketers need to become ROI accountable; yet, according to the report's findings, 73 percent of CEO's believe that marketers lack credibility because they cannot prove in a precise manner the impact of marketing on their business. However, of those CEO's, 70 percent admit that their own lack of trust is to blame for the marketers' poor reputation and lack of expectation of performance, ensuring the continuation of bad marketing performances.

Jerome Fontaine, CEO of Fournaise, stated, "Whether we like it or not, what CEOs are telling us is clear cut: They don't trust traditional marketers, they don't expect much from them. CEOs have to deliver shareholder value. Period. So they want no-nonsense ROI Marketers; they want business performance; they want results. At the end of the day, Marketers have to stop whining about being misunderstood by CEOs, and have to start remembering that their job is to generate customer demand and to deliver performance. This is business.

Hold Your Marketing Accountable

As a business owner or as a marketing consultant your actions are accountable to increase the sales metrics for your company or for those that you consult. People in my field may chastise me for those words, but I can assure you that CEO's and business owners are applauding me right now for writing it. Yes, branding and marketing do not directly sell someone and close deals, but, sooner or later, one has to make sales to stay in business. And David Ogilvy's statement would agree with me: "If it doesn't sell, it isn't creative."

One of my favorite marketing books of all time is *The End of Marketing as We Know It,* by former Coca-Cola CMO, Sergio Zyman. This is a must-read for anyone who needs to learn that this Marketing and Sales disconnect is not new and not an unimportant business phenomenon. In the book Zyman writes, "The goal of advertising is to sell more stuff to more people more often for more money."

Without sales, branding and marketing activities are a futile waste of time, effort and finance. Yet, without effective, intelligent branding and marketing, sales will struggle. Sales and marketing are two peas cut of the same pod, bound in a symbiotic relationship.

All businesses and all of their marketing personnel need to learn *HOW TO SELL,* because *selling fits, technically, under the umbrella of marketing.* Branding and marketing activities need to be monetized. Marketing personnel need to be held accountable for sales results. Branding and marketing has always been much more than just "Massaging our image." Branding and marketing concern themselves with attracting attention, reaching a target audience and generating viable, measurable SALES and profitability for the brand and its backing company.

MORE ABOUT THE MARKETING/ SALES DISCONNECT

Ask any business owner this question: "What do you desire most from your marketing efforts?"

If you surveyed 100 business owners and CEO's randomly in any city of the world, I can assure that the vast majority of them would state higher sales and more new clientele as their top objectives. But, if you surveyed 100 marketers, they would state that they would like to see an increase in:

* Unique website visitors
* New followers
* Numbers of shares and "likes"
* Press coverage
* Industry awards & recognitions
* High praises from their contemporaries
* Beautiful marketing materials

This disconnect needs to be mended and properly organized into seamless functions and structures that enable marketing and sales to work in concert to produce viable, resolved and attained objectives leading to known and attained goals.

THE BUSINESS BROKER

I remember the day I went to visit a successful business broker in the Los Angeles area. I had been referred by a close business associate of mine to speak to him about a marketing strategy for a new high-tech start-up.

After about a half-hour of customary introductions and telling each other who we were and what we do, his tone turned serious, and he got straight to the point: "Edwin, I need to be honest with you. I've worked with a lot of marketing people over the last 20-plus years, and none of them have really done anything positive for me, in terms of results. What makes you different?"

While this question would throw most marketers into a cold sweat, hemming and hawing for the perfect answer, I knew already that this was a concern of all business owners and CEO's. They wrestle with the mere idea of effectively investing their hard-won revenues into marketing.

My answer to this business broker was simple and took less than three minutes: "I reverse engineer the marketing process by starting with the sales team. Then I work backwards, inquiring into what type of branded-content materials and training they most desire to possess, which would help them in their estimation to close more sales. I do not start with the marketing people who tend to sit in their ivory towers, trying to divine the heavens for 'brand image' inspiration."

After my explanation, he told me that no one ever explained the ideal marketing process that simply or effectively. I closed the deal and delivered my program to his company. In 2014, his company experienced significant growth in sales.

Surveys, reverse-engineering and Branded Content 101. I do what works.

Touch Points

"Even in the digital era, our surveys show that personal interactions with sales reps remain the most influential factor—across touch points—for B2B customers. That makes salespeople a great source of information about the degree to which customers see your products as differentiated or worth a premium." - McKinsey & Company

Whether or not this is expressed openly, I can assure you this is how CEO's and business owners will judge you as a marketer. In fact, when all is said and done, there are two questions that you will have to answer and address - head on - to earn someone's business:

1. What do you do? (And they will want specifics in terms of processes, time lines and how you will conduct yourself with them.)
2. What results have you achieved with others? (Specific case studies and KPIs that prove your acumen in elevating customer acquisitions and revenue.)

Any marketing professional that can effectively answer these questions and prove them with fully documented case studies, positive customer reviews and improved sales statistics, will have plenty of new business coming on board.

THE DIFFERENCE BETWEEN SALES AND MARKETING

The difference between Sales and Marketing is an important factor for any business owner or CEO to comprehend, if they are to grow their brand's success.

The lack of solid sales and marketing plans is a top reason why Sales falls short of its goals. As any shortcoming here results in revenue and profitability shortfalls, this area requires intense focus and careful strategic planning by any small business or startup.

Many business owners gravitate toward organizing internal processes to address lowered viability. While this is important, what created explosive growth for some of the largest, most-known brands was their intelligent and consistent branding, marketing, PR and *sales*.

But first, let's look at marketing.

What is the Exact Job of Marketing?

Marketing is media-driven where your paid ad or similar content (landing pages, TV, radio, direct mail, print, etc.) introduces your company to prospective customers. Marketing also can be driven outside of advertising, via multiple channels, including media coverage, email, word of mouth, webinars, podcasts and live events.

An intelligent marketing team, which has properly studied your prospective customer demographics, mindset, habits and ethos, can drive the ultimate success of your marketing strategy. They can take what they have learned and target appropriate marketing messages with savvy media placements pointed to where intended customers are looking or listening.

In this context, the team's marketing purpose is to generate awareness and interest of the targeted consumers in order to have that consumer engage profitably with the business. Such engagement can include a simple following of the brand on social media, requesting to speak to a representative on the phone, ordering online, or walking into a store and making a purchase.

The proactive marketing responsibility is to stay ahead of and be able to predict changes in the needs and desires of target audiences and technological issues; and to help not only Management, but also Sales to discern where opportunities lie by providing them with correct strategy and content.

What is The Exact Job of Sales?

Sales contacts the consumer, keeps them engaged to develop interest and desire and follows that with helpful advice and controlled communications designed to lead to "closed transactions."

The company produces or distributes specific products or services and Sales ensures that the exchange of product/services for valuables such as money takes place.

Sales also develops relationships with ongoing customers and/ or channel partners in order to accomplish repeating transactions. Sales accomplishes its objectives by following up on leads generated from marketing, knocks on doors, visits and presentations to potential clients/customers, overcoming any and all objections, negotiating prices and terms, and, at times, working internally to ensure that customers' orders are filled.

The perspective of Sales is from inside the company outward to potential customers and/or repeat sales. Sales' goal-oriented horizon focuses on this week, this month and this quarter. If Sales does not focus on here-and-now, or the somewhat immediate objectives being met, there may not be revenue this week, month or quarter. This sense of immediacy is another key factor that differentiates sales and marketing.

CHET HOLMES' TWELVE POINTS TO INCREASING SALES

In my humble opinion, Chet Holmes was the greatest sales coach and trainer in history. In his book, *The Ultimate Sales Machine*, Chet focuses squarely on the fundamentals of sales. I cannot recommend this book enough. As well, his videos on YouTube are well worth the watch.

Here are 12 key points from Mr. Holmes epic book:

(1) Make the best use of your limited time.
(2) Institute high standards and individual employee training time.

(3) Hold regular company meetings to inform and train all your employees as a group.

(4) Develop your core story and educate your customer.

(5) Attract and hire superstar performers.

(6) Market to your most ideal prospects.

(7) Always perfect your marketing tactics.

(8) Perfect your sales presentation.

(9) Perfect your company's sales process and lay it down in written policy.

(10) Perfect personal selling skills.

(11) Bond with your client with personalized follow-through and follow-up.

(12) Set aggressive goals, hold people accountable and systematically measure your performance with statistics.

Careful review of these 12 points reveals that this is a complete strategic outline to not only improve sales, but also to dovetail Marketing and Sales into an effective dynamic duo. These are the very exact actions that any C-Level executive or business owner needs to put into place to ensure a functioning symbiotic relationship between Marketing and Sales, which results in continuous company sales growth and expansion.

Hiring outside marketing professionals reduces the C-level executive's control over these twelve points. One can only hope that the hired pros are trained and organized to produce ROI, as this is the reason for retaining their services. In any event, accountability for results must be asserted and maintained.

CHAPTER 17

Audio-Visual
Branded Content

OUTSIDE OF CUSTOMER REVIEWS, THE most important content that any brand should be curating and creating is audio-visual (A/V) content.

A/V - "Using both sight and sound, typically in the form of slides or video and recorded speech or music."

The utilization of audio, video and other visual components within your marketing strategy represents the singular differentiator in your branding and customer acquisition goals. If A/V is your weakest link in your marketing efforts, you're not alone. A mere 22 percent of businesses plan on releasing a video within the next 12 months.

The underlying reason is simple.

Hundreds of small business owners and entrepreneurs interviewed by this author, brought to light an overriding opinion that A/V content is the most difficult branded content to conceptualize and produce. "I have no idea what we would make a video about," and "That's sounds very complicated and expensive" were the most common reasons given for not developing A/V content. Yet, producing and leveraging A/V resources to broaden branding, overall messaging, business appeal and customer base would help them measurably.

The A/V factor – its non-use – is a modern Achilles Heel in the business world, which should awaken you to a really big, competitive opportunity. If A/V content, particularly video content, is such a weakness for most brands today, would that not mean that A/V content has the least competition in your industry or field?

Mastering video content could be the difference that sets your brand apart in a "me-too" world of brands.

"...video (and before that, movies and TV) has driven the culture. That culture-driving ability now belongs to anyone who can make a video that the right people choose to watch." - Seth Godin

We have seen that branding is much more than a logo and your materials plastered with that logo. Branding tells your compelling story. Messaging sent out on many levels intends to build trust, and to creatively shape the thoughts of your target audiences.

Branding seeks interaction with your customers, which proactively builds rapport and brand loyalty — precisely what A/V content can do so well. Audio-visual creativity and content is practically unlimited in this regard. Already app and video-based customer reviews have replaced text-based postings. In the near future, Yelp, Google My Business and similar sites will invite and use A/V content the same way that YouTube created a whole new generation of "YouTubers," who today are a creative and powerful voice.

How will you interact and leverage your branding with A/V? Will you provide courses, "how to" content, case studies, branded entertainment, memes, infographics and podcasts? Or will you wait to see how your old competitors or a new start-up seizes the A/V opportunity before you act?

FROM A TO V

Today in branding, the expression "from A to Z" needs to become "from A to V." Your content should include everything from A to V. Without audio/visual content, which would include video, webinars, podcasts, memes, photographs, SlideShare, infographics and charts, to name a few current choices of venue, you will not make the impact that you need to make. You will not take the lion's share of today's marketplace in your field.

AN A/V EXAMPLE FOR A SMALL BUSINESS

I gave the following idea to *The Lost Bean's* owner. Over the years, the owner and I have become friends and we have discussed a bunch of marketing ideas for his business.

Coffee is the drink of conversation. Since the Revolutionary War, Americans have talked and plotted small and large ventures over cups of coffee. As a national pastime, coffee is older than baseball and, in my opinion, works well with apple pie. (Make mine *a la mode*, please.)

My notion was this: Why not capture that "conversational" spirit of coffee on video by emulating television's most popular genre, the celebrity-chef cooking show? I suggested to the owner that he should produce two-to-three minute videos that would weave the history of coffee among current popular TV chefs or barista's demonstrating how they make the most popular coffee drinks that they serve.

By relating interesting tidbits of the history of coffee, the unique types of coffee and the countries they originate from, hundreds of potential A/V segments of caffeinated content could be produced. Imagine these simple videos being shared among thousands of email followers, posted regularly on social media sites (also potentially re-posted) and embedded as optimized blog posts to be discovered by other local coffee devotee's.

And to make it easier, I suggested to the owner that these could be shot with existing mobile phones or tablets, which almost all of his barista's own. With apps such as Videolicious and Animoto, and animated videos available from GoAnimate, there is no reason that A/V content should be complex, expensive and inaccessible to any small-business owner, entrepreneur, non-profit group, or start-up.

THE STATISTICS ARE CONCLUSIVE

Statistics show that visual content increases your traffic, generates higher conversions from your content and increases sales. Here are just a few:

* Businesses who market with infographics grow in traffic an average of 12% more than those who don't.
* Posts with visuals receive 94 percent more page visits and engagement than those without.
* 60 percent of consumers are more likely to click on a business whose images appear in search results.
* 67 percent of consumers consider clear, detailed images carry more weight than product information or customer ratings.
* Videos increase people's understanding of your product or service by 74 percent.
* YouTube is the No. 2 search engine in the world.
* A third of all online activity is spent watching video.
* The average internet user is exposed to an average of 32.2 videos in a month.

- Every day 100 million internet users watch an online video.
- 50 percent of users watch business-related videos on YouTube once a week.
- 75 percent of users visit the marketer's website after viewing a video.
- 75 percent of executives watch work-related videos on business websites at least once a week.
- An average user spends 16 minutes watching online video ads every month.
- 80 percent of internet users remember the video ads they watch online.
- 26 percent of internet users look for more information after viewing a video ad.
- 22 percent of internet users visit the website named in a video ad they viewed.
- After visiting a video ad, 12 percent of viewers purchase the specific product featured in the ad.
- Website visitors are 64 percent more likely to buy a product on an online retail site after watching a video.
- Real estate listings with videos receive a whopping *403 percent more inquiries* than those without videos.
- Click-through rates increase two to three times when marketers include a video in an email.
- Subscriber-to-lead conversion rates increase 51 percent when video is included in an email marketing campaign.
- 80 percent of your online visitors will watch a video, while only 20 percent will actually read content in its entirety.
- Your website is 50 times more likely to appear on the first page of a search engine results page if it includes video.
- In 30 days more video content is uploaded in 30 days than all three major U.S. TV networks combined have created in 30 years.
- 90 percent of users state that viewing a video about a product is helpful in the decision process.

- 45.5 percent of internet users view at least one video online over the course of a month.
- 45 percent of viewers will stop watching a video after one minute and 60 percent by two minutes.
- 72 hours of video are uploaded to YouTube every minute.
- An introductory company email that includes a video receives an increased click-through rate by 96 percent.

How to Produce Affordable Video Content

If you are challenged and do not know how to begin, here is one powerful tip. Young people have grown up on social media and A/V technology; many of them are studying video production and marketing at local community colleges or universities. A few may be the next Steven Spielberg. All need to build a portfolio. Let them build their future career and portfolio by creating video content (and podcasts) for you. For pennies on the dollar compared to professional crews, hire these bright and talented individuals within your community and let them create great visual content for you.

Let's Not Forget Audio Content: Podcasting

Audio content may be considered the lesser of content within the A/V world; nevertheless, it is content that can create a valuable experience. It is an effective method for reaching more potential clientele. Audio content is perfect for use on home computers, mobile devices, and while driving.

According to a recent Edison Research Study on the Podcast Consumer, awareness of podcasting has grown 105 percent since 2006 from 22 percent in 2006 to 45 percent in 2012. Likewise, the percentage of consumers indicating they have listened to an audio podcast has grown 163 percent from 11 percent in 2006 to 29 percent in 2012.

Jeff Bullas (www.jeffbullas.com) points out, "So why is podcasting having a resurrection? It is due to two key factors. 1. The growth and rapid adoption of smart phones. You can now get your podcast direct to your phone without having to hook up your iPod to the computer. 2. The explosive growth of an online media portal where you can publish and download your podcasts.... called 'iTunes.' These have provided the device and the channel to make podcasting effective, efficient and able to be distributed with ease that was only imagined years ago."

An easy way to create audio content is to convert from your videos, your blog posts and written presentations into audio recordings that can be rendered as podcasts. One can also convert audio content, such as live phone interviews and existing videos, into audio podcasts.

An important element of created audio content is that you are telling your story to one person at a time, no matter how many end-users consume your audio content.

KEY PODCAST MARKETING TIPS
* Optimize your podcast for search engines with keyword-rich title, description and meta data.
* Optimize it for iTunes search.
* Create artwork that has a professional-quality book cover.
* Ensure that your share buttons are included.
* Offer valuable insight, know-how, resources, and "how-to" tips.
* Include interviews of contemporary industry leaders.

* Include or broadcast "calls to action" within your podcast.
* Link your podcasts to landing pages for easier purchasing or joining.
* Syndicate your podcasts to popular podcast directories.

Audio-Visual content is a must-have branding method for any **Power Brand** that is serious about dominating the attention and interaction of their target audience.

CHAPTER 18

Mobile Marketing and Your Power Brand

PEOPLE ARE MOBILE ENTITIES. So, of course, mobile marketing is founded upon the fact that, as a species, we are nomadic. We all suffer from wanderlust. Some of us travel vast distances to sightsee, hike or ski. For most, strolling down a busy street, walking in a park, going for a run or riding down some mountain highway on a motorcycle is enough. Your branding and marketing must resonate with the wanderlust instinct in all of us.

Mobile – "Able to move or be moved freely or easily. Capable of moving or changing quickly from one state or condition to another." [Latin mobilis, from *movibilis*, from movere, *to move*]

Mobile marketing is no longer for big brands only. Mobile marketing has become an important platform for the marketing strategy of any small business. It's great for securing business with local customers on-the-go. The small business marketing crowd increasingly leverages this reality: customers aren't sitting at a home on a computer any longer, searching for local businesses; instead, they are mobile, and so are the devices on which they search businesses. Almost 70 percent of all emails are now read on a mobile device.

THE NOWNESS OF CONSUMERISM

The Nowness of Consumerism dictates being able to connect with your clients at the very moment they want to find general or specific information about your particular brand. The internet has spoiled and empowered consumers to be able to access desired information on their terms, whenever and wherever they want that information. **Power Brands** have to move *very* fast in today's world.

Most primary websites are not mobile friendly today, which is a grave error, but this is changing as Google is now being clear on this matter: if you want your site to rank well, it must be mobile responsive. Adding this feature should be the first part of your mobile marketing to remedy.

LOOK AROUND

You don't have to look very far to find someone pre-occupied with a Smartphone or a tablet in a public place. The same can be seen daily at home, with today's use of portable tablets. Although tablets and mobile devices have taken over the internet market, very few small business brands have yet to cash in on this trend. The numbers don't lie:

* 70 percent of mobile searches lead to online action within an hour.
* 4 out of 5 consumers use smart phones to shop.
* 75 percent of Americans admit to bringing their phone to the bathroom.
* By 2016, mobile is predicted to overtake desktop Internet usage.

When four out of five consumers are using Smartphones to shop, the time to jump onto the mobile marketing gold rush is now. Even more staggering is that 70 percent of mobile searches lead to online action *within the hour*. Not optimizing content for mobile means losing out on a large source of new business and revenue.

The implication is that the same kind of real-time connection and thinking needs to be applied to how we create content. Simply writing short content will not be a viable strategy for long. Briefly put, your content strategy needs to be mobile — "capable of moving or changing quickly from one condition to another."

Markets, the needs and the means of reaching, connecting with, and providing those needs to the market, are changing fast. Some things to consider when creating mobile content are these:

- The reading level of your target audience.
- Short, powerful headlines pull people in.
- Ensuring that your first paragraphs engage and hook the person to read further.
- Make apropos videos that offer useful, helpful data, but are no longer than three minutes in length.
- Keep your designs simple and easy to navigate.
- Make your calls-to-action easy to identify and engage with, such as your phone number.
- Include social media share buttons in your key content.
- Incorporate QR codes into your content that will reach mobile users.

Brands can leverage mobile marketing to make buying experiences easier for their customers, whether a one-click checkout on any e-commerce site online or the ability to click a button on one's phone just before walking out of a physical store. The brands that fully embrace the utility of mobile payments will be big winners in the end.

The future of marketing is mobile. Mobile is the most personal device we possess, which makes it the best device to market to, and, for some parts of the world, mobile devices are the first and only computer people will ever possess.

CHAPTER 19

How to Properly Repurpose and Curate Your Content

WHEN A BUSINESS PERSON OR marketing team decides to write out a strategy to create branded content, overwhelm can soon follow, making them stumble. *How are we going to create all this content with limited time and financial resources?* is the loudest cry. And the answer is *to* repurpose and *curate content.*

Repurpose: "To find a new use for an idea, product, or asset." [From Old French from *porposer* "to put forth."]

Curate: "To pull together, sift through, and select for presentation, as music or website content; to act as a curator; curator." [From Medieval Latin *c r tus,* from *c ra* spiritual oversight, cure]

Understanding the definitions of *repurpose* and *curate* refocuses your number one challenge to *How can I compete with bigger brands that have writers, staff and young people managing their social media?*

Admittedly, the challenge can overwhelm the newcomer to branded content. But, the strategy of creating core content and repurposing and curating it rises to this problem's solution.

In the content marketing world, to *repurpose* means to reuse your content from one medium to another full or partial use on another medium. Mastery of repurposing enables the increase of content output by 200 to 500 percent without much additional effort, resources or inspiration required.

Before getting into the finer details and actions of how to repurpose content, here is a simple overview of repurposing you can interact with:

Write a 500-word blog post containing creative and insightful data about a product or service. Once written and posted, repurpose that blog into a short YouTube video. Factually, your blog post may contain so much information from which you could produce several videos from that one blog post.

Well, what about 20-30 tweets from that same blog post?

The audio part of your YouTube video could again be repurposed into a podcast.

You could take selective quotes from the original video transcript and convert them into 20 small posts or tweets on social media channels. And these tweets may be spread out over a period of days... all linking back to the original blog post.

Over time, let's say you write 50 or 100 blog posts. All of this information can be collected and repurposed into an eBook, an actual book, company brochures and other types of content. That would be repurposing at its finest.

By repurposing content, you will be able to vary your content, plus make it appear like an endless stream of new content.

EVERGREEN CONTENT

Content that effectively works for your brand, season after season, year after year, with little or no need for upkeep is called "Evergreen Content."

The best part of such content is that, once created, you can promote it endlessly. You can cross-promote evergreen videos by embedding them on your blog site. You can embed your video presentations on your LinkedIn profile, put up a podcast on iTunes and other channels, and place the content on social networks as photos on Instagram, motivational quotes on Facebook, quick tips on Twitter, and so much more.

Repurposing your core content increases visibility, improves reach, and opens your content to views on computers, tablets, and mobile phones. Repurposing content creates an impression that you are everywhere at once, and with far less effort than creating new content.

Moreover, your evergreen content stays on the web for months and years to be found by future customers looking for what you have to offer and share. Evergreen content works for your *Power Brand* 24/7.

HOW TO BEGIN YOUR REPURPOSING STRATEGY

Action No. 1 – Determine the principal product or service you want to market... maybe a solution or benefit to feature, such as a case study. For example, a business coach desires to promote a specific workshop on self-confidence and motivation, knowing that his target audiences are sales professionals and entrepreneurs.

Action No. 2 – List out in writing 20-30 benefits to be gained from your workshop on self-confidence and motivation. Here would be some simple examples. [How to...]:

* Remain motivated during economic stress.
* Be self-confident.
* Increase your self-confidence in your new career search.
* Stay motivated when your customers say "no."
* Learn what kills a salesperson's motivation.
* Stay confident when fielding sales objections.
* Avoid losing confidence around women.
* Motivate your employees to be more productive.
* Not lose your self-confidence in your abilities as a leader.

The above are examples of how a core idea – "Self-confidence & Motivation" – can be developed into many variations for marketing purposes.

Action No. 3 – From the listed benefits (titles), create content around each. While these will mainly be blog posts, videos, podcasts, webinars and other types of content can also be developed from them.

HOT TIP: If you are writing blog posts, be sure to include relevant photos, infographics and internet links.

Action No. 4 – Now take your blog post and convert into a video. Perhaps, you could take the general points of a blog post and summarize them.

If the blog post was titled, "The 7 Rules of Motivating Your Sales", you could take your 800-word blog post and summarize these seven points within two to three minutes in a video. Also, upload onto YouTube and link back to your website, ensuring that you optimize your video and blog with keywords and pertinent, written content.

I suggest that if you are not familiar with how to create a video or know how to optimize it, find someone in our area that is an expert in video marketing. This is a field exploding within the marketing world, so it should not be difficult to find competent professionals in your area.

Action No. 5 – Break your content up into small bits and share these on Twitter, LinkedIn and Facebook.

For example, I could take a blog post about "23 Ways a Small Business Can Promote" and break away each as a daily tip sent out on my social-media pages. The result? 23 individual tweets and posts. The same can be done with my key sentences that convey important ideas. Perhaps, there would be ten to twenty tweets in one blog post or the transcript of a YouTube video.

The point is that you have an endless of supply of tweets and daily posts that you can manufacture. There is no limit but your imagination.

You can retweet these key ideas and quotes monthly. Imagine this: 150 key sentences and quotes can be five tweets per day for an entire month!

The major key is to link your original blog post, video or other content it came from in later tweets and posts, driving more people to your blog post and website.

Action No. 6 – Become an author. 20,000 — 40,000 accumulated words from among your previous blog posts and videos, can be combined into a repurposed product - a book or eBook capable of positioning you as an expert and thought leader in your industry. Authors today are still looked up to as authorities. Handing someone your book impresses more than giving them your business card, regardless of the card's design and appearance.

More Options

You can hire a ghostwriter to turn all your posts into a book or an eBook, if you cannot see yourself writing it. Professional ghostwriters can be found, who are not only quite competent, but also capable of guiding you through the process of research, writing and indie-publishing. You can check search engines for reliable and competent ghostwriters in your area. If you're on a super-tight budget, check with local colleges and universities for students majoring in writing. Here are two, experienced resources:

- Ronald Joseph Kule (ronkulebooks.com) - internationally published author, biographer, ghost-writer, editor and small publisher (KuleBooks LLC).
- Elance.com - a platform for freelance writers and writing opportunities.

Action No. 7 – Look into how your content can be further repurposed. Can you make a slideshow presentation for workshops? Can you place your videos on your website on a page dedicated to all the videos you have created? How can you take positive reviews on Yelp and share them on your other social-media channels? Or gather all the best things that people have said or written about you and place them on a dedicated "5-Star Review" page on your website?

The possibilities are only limited by your creativity and your understanding of the types of content with which one can create and repurpose.

FURTHER ACTIONS THAT CREATE REPURPOSED CONTENT

There a few other actions I wanted to list, because there are so many options and opportunities today to repurpose your content with all the available formats. It is important to discover the ones that make sense to you.

Online learning is a growing trend. There are sites popping up that can help you find a new home for the content you've worked so hard to create. Here are some of the most popular:

* Udemy
* Skillshare
* Guides.co

Slidedecks is an excellent way to reach business people and decision makers. Why not create a great slideshow with some of the excellent content that you are creating? If you do, there are several places where you can share your newly created content.

* Slideshare
* Slideworld
* SlideBloom
* Scribd

Infographics... visual representations of information, data or knowledge intended to present complex information quickly and clearly... is a fun way to create, share, and consume content.

What if you converted a few of your posts (especially how-to posts) into handy infographics or visual-content marketing?

* Visual.ly
* Picktochart
* Infogr.am
* Infoactive

The following are a set of tools that not too many people know exist. These sites will take a quote that you have and turn it into a beautiful image that you can share on social media. The ease of creating and sharing content makes these tools effective for marketers that post frequently.

* Recite
* Quozio
* Quotescover

Although memes (A **meme** is "an idea, behavior, or style that spreads from person to person within a culture".) can be overly informal, they can be a good way to connect with audiences, if used strategically. Just make sure that you use good taste as incorrectly using a meme can lead to public ridicule.

* Imgflip
* MemeCenter
* Quickmeme

CURATED CONTENT: A *POWER BRAND* STRATEGY

Curating content adds depth, perspective and, most importantly, value around your own brand's content. Curated content keeps your brand front and center without the unnecessary time and efforts of having to re-create them.

What, then, is "curated content?"

"Content curation is the act of continually identifying, selecting and sharing the best and most relevant online content and other online resources (and by that I mean articles, blog posts, videos, photos, tools, tweets, or whatever) on a specific subject to match the needs of a specific audience." – Ann Handley

"Content Curation is a term that describes the act of finding, grouping, organizing or sharing the best and most relevant content on a specific issue." - Rohit Bhargava

For a long time, content curation was largely a marketing tool for selecting appropriate information for corporate blogs or websites, depending on the company's niche or business sector. Also, as a tool for selecting content for brands to post to social media channels. Examples, check out curata.com, Scoop.it or Trapit.

However, recently curated content has begun to see wider applications among end-users eager to cut down on the time they spend every day sifting through online information. The technology of curation allows for the creation of online newspapers or magazines, like Paper.li, or pages like Storify, which lets the user create stories or timelines using social media such as Twitter, Facebook and Instagram.

CURATION VERSUS CREATION
The major difference in content creation versus content curation is who generates the content that you are sharing. Content curation is pulling content from multiple sources and then channeling these into one platform or piece of content, such as an email or a blog post. Being a source of curated content can position you as someone to turn to for answers, since you are showcasing your ability to feature such a wide array of valuable insight and information.

Such positioning increases your value to a wider audience of followers, leading to more connections and, in turn, potentially greater interaction and, eventually, more sales and income.

If you cannot decide which direction to go, creating or curating, you can do a little of both. Create content with blog posts, videos, webinars and more. As well, curate content from the web, Facebook, Twitter and LinkedIn and send these stories as links on your next email, such as, for example, "The Best News and Views About _____."

Content curation gives any brand, small business person, entrepreneur, and non-profit a wonderful way to connect with people without the worry of having to create 100 percent of the content they share to their target audiences.

EXAMPLES OF CURATED CONTENT
It is completely real to me that "curated content" can be a new and even difficult concept to wrap one's wits around and to have it settle in as something comprehensible. Some examples, actual and fictional, may help to clarify this branding and marketing technique.

* ACTUAL: The *Drudge Report* run by Matt Drudge is one of the most popular news sites online. Catering to the conservative side of the political spectrum, the *Drudge Report* consists of a set of links to third-party news content that has been editorialized by their internal team. The *Drudge Report* is now one of the most popular news websites online.
* ACTUAL: One of most well-known examples of curation is Digg. Digg had over 3.8 million visitors per month and millions of registered users as of 2012. Every day, millions of users submit interesting content to Digg and collectively vote or "Digg" content, raising the voted-best content to the top.

As a result, Digg has grown into one of the most popular content sites on the internet solely by curating third-party content.

- ACTUAL: *Clinical Advisor* is a closed circulation magazine serving the physician assistant and nurse practitioner market. Their challenge was how to get video content to readers without expending content-creation dollars they didn't have to support advertising. Originally, they looked at trying to shoot their own videos and building a studio, but other publications warned them away — the cost of original production for B2B sites was simply prohibitive. Content curation really allowed them to gather a lot of videos, and create a really robust channel very quickly.

- ACTUAL: Reddit (reddit.com) is the place you go for uncommon and unheard of stories and conversations that you otherwise may never know about or read. Reddit uses crowdsourcing to produce interesting, serious, and silly content that keeps readers hooked.

- ACTUAL: I met a brighter-than-average CPA at one of my marketing workshops, who told me that he has curated and shared articles from various media channels to his LinkedIn wall. He has done so consistently, posting three to four articles daily. He added that he has attracted and boarded many new clients who view him as an expert because they see that he is relevant and on top of important issues in his field.

- FICTIONAL: A winery could curate the best stories on wine; videos about the types of wines available; and could, as an ongoing exercise, educate their clientele and new visitors to the world of fine wines.

- FICTIONAL: A financial advisor could share articles and featured stories from well-respected journals, magazines and blogs via his email. By showcasing the wide variety of news on investment trends, and his willingness to share these data, he would position himself as a well-rounded and non-biased source of investment information.

* FICTIONAL: If I owned a motorcycle shop, I would feature the hundreds of videos and reviews about the new bikes released each year. As well, I would curate and feature motorcycle events, "how to" information, product reviews on equipment, including motorcycle races from around the world.

* FICTIONAL: A medium or large business regional contractor could curate all of the DIY information surrounding home improvement. Home improvement TV shows are in popular demand, and these deliver, for the most part, curated content. A regional contractor could tap into that enthusiasm and interest and feature its company as the "go to" resource for curated content on all DIY projects. This could be sent out as an email or as key articles featured on a daily blog. Short DIY videos could be curated and shared on a company YouTube channel and other media, further positioning the brand as an authority.

Repurposing and curating content is an important and impressive tactic to deploy for any **Power Brand** looking to engage and educate their target audiences by providing a wide array of relative content by repurposing and curating it. Your brand will no longer be a static entity, but one that communicates, shares, and connects with the real interests of people.

CHAPTER 20
It's All about Audience

MOST BRANDS GET SO WRAPPED up in their own message and mission that they lose sight of why they exist as a company - *to identify with, sell to, and service customers.* Branding's success is ultimately and completely dependent on the support of an audience or a number of audiences.

Most professionals, with whom I discuss the subject of audiences fall into three camps:

1. The individual who has not truly considered their audience(s) as an important factor.
2. The individual who already "knows everything" about his audience(s), but their knowledge is not based on actual market research.
3. The individual who has a deep grasp of audience(s) due to thorough research.

There is a great book on this subject of audience. I suggest that you purchase and read *Audience: Marketing in the Age of Subscribers, Fans & Followers*", by Jeffrey K. Rohrs. Under 250 pages of reading, you'll gain a deep understanding of how to build and service an audience.

"Your purpose is to make your audience see what you saw, hear what you heard, feel what you felt. Relevant detail, couched in concrete, colorful language, is the best way to recreate the incident as it happened and to picture it for the audience." - Dale Carnegie

BRANDING AND YOUR AUDIENCE

While you are working on all your elements of branding and the creation of your branded content you will need to spend as much time and effort, or more, building up a number of genuine contacts, followers and fans. Great content distributed to 100 people will not be as effective is that exact same content distributed to 100,000 genuine people.

Audience development and the generation of more contacts, loyal followers and fans, are as *vitally* important as your branding and your content-creation efforts. When it comes to developing and proactively growing a genuine audience, size absolutely matters. Your most important audience factors are:

* Number of email contacts
* Number of genuine social media followers (Facebook, LinkedIn, Twitter, Instagram, Google+, etc.)
* Number of likes, shares, retweets and video views
* Number of attendees to webinars, seminars and workshops
* Number of website visitors
* Number of positive impressions within media

When all of these are increasing, and those audiences are consuming more of your engaging content, an increased amount of inbound leads, phone calls, walk-ins, online orders and actual sales will eventually result.

Your branding and marketing planning must include *how* you are going to increase your number of contacts and followers; otherwise, you'll sweat to create a ***Power Brand*** and Branded Content but wonder why very few are interested in what you have to say or offer.

BEST METHOD TO ATTRACT NEW IDENTITIES
To quote the Red Hot Chili Peppers, "Give it away now."

On the homepage of your website and in routine offers in your social media posts, you can attract new followers and email identities by giving things away. In marketing, these giveaways are called "freemiums."

Freemiums can be free reports, eBooks, eCourses, access to membership, or any similar offer that would be considered of value to your target audience. A floral shop could offer a free guide on how to grow plants more successfully. A bridal shop could offer a free wedding-planner guide. An author could give away the first three chapters of his latest book. These giveaways do not need to be very expensive or lengthy, but they should be professionally designed and packaged so that, when they are downloaded or received, they create a perception of high value.

> "Audience development requires either of these tactics: target a specific group and bet on it catalyzing scale; or target a larger, less specific group and bet on some portion doing business and spreading it. For content online (including video), audience development is part of the equation now more than ever before, since there is just so much content "out there". - Forbes

Audience development is a vitally important strategy and activity for any ***Power Brand.***

CHAPTER 21

Amplifying Your Power Brand with Power Influencers

INFLUENCER - "A PERSON OR thing with the capacity or power to have an effect on someone or something." [Latin *influere*, from *in-* 'into' +*fluere* 'to flow'.]

"Influencer" marketing can be defined as the form of marketing that identifies and targets specific individuals which possess influence over your potential customers and followers. An influencer is not necessarily an individual or a brand with a lot of followers on social media.

Value is determined by expertise on a subject, and the relationship and interaction between that influencer and their followers. In the past, brands may have focused on popular bloggers and celebrities, but today there is a new wave of "everyday" consumers and authorities capable of making a similar impact for your brand.

We are seeing a significant growth in the importance of influencer marketing due to a dispersal of consumer attention, stemming from a plethora of media channels. Now, instead of a television-centered attention span, the consumer's attention is spread across many digital channels and majorly focused on social networks.

YouTube and Instagram enjoy a large share of the influencer-marketing spend, but social platforms – Vine, Pinterest and Snapchat, etc. – are beginning to reap larger portions of advertisers' budgets. Influencer marketing works, because social media allows for word-of-mouth marketing at scale.

Like yourself, I have been introduced to many new brands, products, and services through my expanding circle of friends, followers and formal internet contacts, whom I also follow on social media.

ONLINE RELATIONSHIP BUILDING

Building a relationship with a mere handful of online influencers can create a significant impact on your business's growth. Online influencers have dynamic personalities and they create impact with them. They command respect from other key players within their industries and they have attentive followings.

Second only to your customer base, relationships with influencers are requisite for success. They can and do shape the attitudes and decisions of consumers by popularizing certain products and ideas. By sharing your content across multiple channels, they can make a huge difference in your brand's status.

The best news is that many top influencers also happen to be accessible, even when you think it would be impossible to find a connection with one of them.

(Later on in this section, I'm going to give you some tips on how to connect and effectively engage with power influencers.)

I once read a study that 60 percent of web content is created or shared by only five percent of those active on the web and social media. Similar to the concept of the 80/20 rule (80 percent of your revenue comes from 20 percent of your audience), the bulk of content created and shared comes from a small band of influencers sometimes called, "Amplifiers", "Thought Leaders" and "Evangelists."

Within your industry and circles, you need to locate and render VIP service and status to these influential people. They may be key opinion leaders, avid followers, best customers, or all of that and more. Find who moves the needle, who is listened to, or who loves to share content obsessively, and woo those influencers onto your side; get them to share your content. You can best connect with these influencers in person at mixers and industry events. To make connections with them online, I have found that Twitter and LinkedIn are my two most effective, social media platforms.

Social media activity means connecting, conversing and communicating as a genuine person. This three-step sequence I refer to as "Influencer C Cubed," or simply, **IC³.**

1. Contact
2. Connect
3. Collaborate

On the Contact step, you identify who is the best influencer for your industry or niche for you, someone with whom you can connect. You should establish a number, with whom you plan to contact.

Once you contact them you employ the Connect step. Your intention is to build rapport. You begin by following them online, at times commenting on their content when you can be genuine about it. If you can, connect with them offline as well. Connect with influencers in person as much as possible.

Once you have established a mutual rapport, you will work to establish collaborations on marketing initiatives and programs. Be sure to promote your goal, which is to increase brand awareness and client acquisition for you and them. Assisting the influencer to gain more exposure and clout will bring a natural reciprocation with your brand.

INFLUENCERS AND KEYWORDS

Before you start your influencer discovery trail, avoid the mistake of shooting from the hip and scattering yourself all over. Instead, search for influencers by following your top SEO keywords. Think more from the point of view of who *you* want to influence. What topics will be important to them? What questions will they have during the sales cycle; and what do you really know about their preferences for information discovery, consumption and interaction?

Careful insight (in combination with SEO keywords) will guide you toward a more productive search for influencers that could make a difference for you, whom you also help.

TIPS ON REACHING AND ENGAGING INFLUENCERS

- Use LinkedIn to establish contacts. Using social media will often be the fastest, easiest way to connect with online influencers, because they are already active within these established platforms. They share the same purpose to connect with like-minded individuals. LinkedIn is a useful place to start, since it is the largest B2B network online.
- Leverage Twitter to establish contacts. Twitter's "verified" status feature lets others know who the influencers are. But, even if this status is not yet attained or apparent, most people

handle their own Twitter account, avoiding the need to get past a gatekeeper.

* Use sites like Klout and Twello to identify the reaches and followings of key influencers.

* Study industry leaders within your niche, who are moving the needle and creating positive waves. They appear in industry journals, blogs, and publications as well as at live events, where they may be featured speakers. Make it a point to know who they are and then contact them. Overcome any shyness on your part. Remember, they share your purpose to contact and connect with like-minded people.

* When utilizing social media channels to reach out and contact influencers, don't merely introduce yourself and leave it at that. Offer something to interact upon; perhaps an interview with the targeted person, which can be done by email or telephone, albeit ideally over a cup of coffee. Let them know your purpose for the interview: you want to post their success story on your blog. You may also want to have them consider mentoring you. Successful people usually love helping genuine individuals to grow and learn.

* Guest blogging is effective for getting your name and brand in front of influencers. Locate relevant bloggers through a search on Google or via sites like Technorati. Your first inclination will be to want to connect with the most influential bloggers in your industry or niche, but you should look at a few less-famous bloggers first. Having your content published on smaller blogs can escalate you to larger ones after you have published content to show to an influencer.

* Ask for referrals and introductions to other influencers. Online or offline, getting introduced to someone influential by a mutual friend walks you into their circle with "transferred trust." Just make sure that the introduction comes with a prior agreement to meet you, not by surprise, which may be construed as

an ambush. The person facilitating the connection should speak highly of you, so that the transfer of trust is established. A strong verbal validation will accomplish this end.

* Predetermine what value you can bring to the table. Offer your assistance for free. When you finally do connect with an influencer, you will need to come to the table with a clear understanding of your value proposition. And your best bet is to make it irresistible. Depending upon your existing skill sets and resources, this can vary widely. When you bring a clearly established value to an influential person, you open the door to new opportunities for them and you.

Do these several actions well and you will have access to the influencers you choose… and to their acumen, their help, and their established network of followers and connections.

INVEST IN YOUR CUSTOMER BASE

Even if only a handful of your customers are actual influencers, treat them all as important, unique individuals. Your potential and actual audiences are your brand's most valuable assets. Each and every one of them know that they have plenty of other choices in this consumer-driven economy, so be kind and service their needs with courtesy. You never know whether or not they will one day become an influencer, or which ones they will come to know.

Every time you invest your intelligence, know-how, effort, care, attention, services, and your heart and soul into your customers, influencers, shareholders, followers and/or employees, payback will be represented by reciprocal efforts on their part to help others discover your amazing **Power Brand**. We live, after all, in "**The Age of Search**", so let your audience discover the best of your brand through inspired influencers, who will tell others where to find you.

CHAPTER 22

Social Media and Branded Content

BECAUSE SOCIAL MEDIA IS SO accessible to everyone and is relatively free to leverage, it appears to be a free-for-all marketing opportunity, which does not require planning and thoughtful articulation. Anyone can work with it, and one can post the most random thoughts or content limited only by the imagination. However, while one can suppose that this is how to implement social-media marketing, that notion would be quite limited; nothing could be further from the truth, when building your ***Power Brand***.

Let's get a better insight into social media by reviewing three definitions:

"Social media is all about leveraging online tools that promote sharing and conversations, which ultimately lead to engagement with current and future customers and influencers in your target market. The key to social media working is having a content marketing strategy that involves the distribution of valuable, relevant and compelling content that promotes the behavior you are looking for that will ultimately drive your business. Most businesses start with the tools. Effective social media starts with a content strategy that helps to position you and your brand as the expert in your niche through provocative, informative and helpful content. Then, once that is accomplished, the social media tools are now available today that make the plan come together." - Joe Pulizzi, Content Marketing Institute

"Media for social interaction, using highly accessible and scalable communication techniques. Social media is the use of web-based and mobile technologies to turn communication into interactive dialogue." – Wikipedia

"Social media is a communication channel which is very popular, extremely fast, and broad in reach. It has proven itself to be highly effective, as well as trusted by billions of people on Earth, to share and discover relevant content concerning individuals, brands, events, locations and applicable know-how." - Edwin Dearborn

It is quite easy to become bedazzled by the proliferation of social media within our world, as well as how fast it is moving. Factually, nothing confuses more business professionals and entrepreneurs than how to effectively utilize and manage social media as a branding channel. But if you look within the first definition, as provided by Joe Pulizzi, you will see a key datum that leads to a better understanding of how best to utilize social media.

The cornerstone of social media success is *the firm foundation of an effective content strategy*. Too many brands and brand-building business people get this wrong. They build their lists of followers and expose their brands on social media without placing intriguing content on those communication channels. To put it plainly, without something important or interesting to share, what the heck are they sending across time and space via social media? And why?

SOCIAL MEDIA CROSSES MANY MEDIA

Among the rare branding opportunities and chameleon-like attributes that social media possesses is its ability to fit all of your strategies and tactics within four categories most relevant to your brand's quest for success:

* Advertising
* Marketing
* Public Relations
* Customer Service

Social media introduces your brand, its services and its products through advertising, which introduces your prospective and current customers to your offer.

Social media also allows you to market your brand through your customers' "buying experiences" (their sales journey), which include offers of helpful content, how-to tutorials, key benefits explanations, and the actual values that these bring into their lives.

Social media creates and maintains good relationships (Public Relations) with your followers. Its stories, current news, curated content and other relevant information continuously builds trust, and informs about your brand's accomplishments, and how yours continues to serve its community by communicating its core values to members.

Social media is now an integral and vital tool for application of customer service. In particular, Twitter and Yelp have become important, real-time customer-service platforms capable of tracking complaints or requests, to ensure that rapid attention is given to customers who feel alienated by your brand's fulfillment processes.

Social media serves another customer service purpose: it features and distributes "how to" content that enables people to better understand and utilize your products and services.

Social Media and Customer Relationship Management (CRM)

Social media inevitably will become a brand battlefield filled with haters and outspoken complainers. No matter how much you endeavor to make your business ideal and flawless, someone will receive a level of service deem to be poor. And sometimes they will be correct in their complaints, although others will attack you out of spite, jealousy or a myriad of anti-social reasons or traits. When this occurs, realize that the world has a small percentage of contentious, vindictive-by-nature personalities which, largely, can be serviced, but also ignored without lingering harm to your business or reputation.

Every great brand, even the most powerful, has to deal with haters and complainers routinely, but genuine *Power Brands* respond to them in a unique manner: they take the high road with a simple acknowledgement or an offhand dismissal of the most spurious claims.

Certainly there is one caveat for handling anti-social personalities: how you will deal with these people and their purported upsets needs to be a part of your social-media strategic plan, excluding avoidance or cowering in fear when confronted by one.

Social Habit (socialhabit.com), a social-media research group, conducted a study on how consumers interact with brands regarding their customer-service needs and responses to their complaints. Here are some interesting numbers that they found:

- 42 percent expect a response within 60 minutes of their complaint
- 32 percent expect a response within 30 minutes of their complaint

This begs the question: Is your company prepared to handle social media inquiries within one hour? Most companies are not, creating a big gap between their customers' expected response time and their ability to provide an adequate response.

As a result, social interaction should be an integral part of your customer-service policies and procedures. Good business owners have a plan in place to react and communicate; better owners plan for proactive communication and action. A strategic, well-thought-out, social media content strategy can create enhanced customer loyalty, when executed correctly.

"Social media is about the people. Not about your business. Provide for the people and the people will provide for you." – Matt Goulart

The several reasons and scenarios listed represent examples of why strategic planning is so crucial to the HOW's and WHY's of not only your branded content, but also the leveraging of social media capabilities to help your brand's image, as well as meeting or exceeding customer expectations.

ANALYZING THE SOCIAL SIGNALS OF YOUR COMPETITORS

Social media is an incredible looking glass that enables perception about how people feel, what verbiage (keywords) and tone they prefer to express, and their personal needs and interests.

Social media not only distributes your content, but also conducts real-time analytics, alerting you to how the marketplace is moving and shifting and what it seeks from information, product and service resources. When tapped into, social media can alert you to emerging markets, opportunities and new customers about as fast as any other media.

SOCIAL MEDIA AND THE ACTUAL MEDIA

In *The American Journalist in the Digital Age,* journalism professors Lars Willnat and David Weaver surveyed 1,080 U.S. journalists online in the fall of 2013. Theirs is the most recent in a series of reports produced in roughly 10-year increments since 1971 about the behaviors and beliefs of U.S. journalists.

Obviously, one of the major shifts between the last survey in 2002 and the most recent report has been the impact of the Internet on reporters. Social media is a major part of that shift: 40 percent of journalists said social media networks are "very important" to their work and over a third said they spend between 30 and 60 minutes each day on social networking sites.

Social sites, such as Twitter, were by far the most popular type of social media used by journalists. Over half of those surveyed said they regularly use the platform for gathering information and reporting stories.

A national survey conducted in 2009, by Cision and Don Bates of The George Washington University's Master's Degree Program in Strategic Public Relations found that an overwhelming majority of reporters and editors depend on social media sources when researching their stories today. Among the journalists surveyed, 89 percent said they turn to blogs for story research, 65 percent to social-media sites.

If you are attempting to get press coverage for your **Power Brand,** your blogging and social media activity need to be in the mix. Reporters and writers can be sent to your blog and news-related content directly through Twitter, bypassing email spam filters and editors. Blogging and social media, wielded correctly, can help your **Power Brand** gain feature coverage on news channels and outlets.

THE DEBACLE OF 2008

2008 and the financial freefall most of us went through remains a bitter taste in the mouth. Few of us experienced the drop unscathed. Blood was in the water.

Well, I, too, felt the wrath of that financial tsunami, but my ship has finally found calmer seas. To a large degree, social media kept me afloat. Social media became my champion marketing channel that lead me to recover and find renewed success.

In the past four years, business people often have asked me, "Is social media really a viable source of connections, new business and revenue?"

I reply with an unequivocal "YES!" Social media is a viable and powerful communication line to reach people and to convert them into strong, long-lasting relationships, and viable revenue. This has been my network to fall back on and it has redeemed my investments in it in more ways than ever I could have imagined.

Because of social media, my wife and I have very handsome careers, as well as other exciting business and investment projects for our immediate futures, which look very bright, indeed. Our social media marketing efforts will remain a viable part of our retirement planning for a long time to come.

THE SCRAMBLE OF 2009

When the economic collapse of a half a decade ago set in, I witnessed too many people scrambling, pulling back, and hunkering down. At first, to some degree, I boarded that sinking ship. However, lacking resources and ample time, I knew that I had to re-engineer myself and my future business strategies. I did not freak out or go into apathy, I went to work. I reached out to a friend immersed in the tides of the online world and began my latest voyage on the seas of website development, social media and blogging.

I built my social media success by creating and sharing insightful and useful content. After all, meaningless content would be, well, meaningless.

EFFECTIVE SOCIAL-MEDIA PERSPECTIVE

Let's break down branding and social media into a simplistic, yet effective perspective:

Your Brand - That which communicates and offers a unique value.

Your Brand's Intellect – Your branding and marketing strategy.

Your Brand's Anatomy – Your branded content, as well as your products and services.

Your Brand's Value – Your branded content distributed to the audience(s) that results in consumption of your services and products.

In fact, social media is just one group of several important content distribution channels, albeit a powerful way to distribute your content; one that can no longer be ignored or played around with in an amateur manner.

"Social media is a contact sport." – Margaret Molloy

You will need to develop a brand-marketing strategy to succeed with social media. This is why one of the first questions that I ask of those whom I coach is, "Can I see your written marketing strategy?" When they cannot produce one, I know that they will eventually tell me how they are struggling to make their social media perform for them.

Social media without relevant and shared, consumable content is awkward and out of place. Here's how it usually goes: sooner or later, you'll be asking yourself or someone else, "What should we post or tweet?"

Everyone then stares at each other bewildered, because two prior steps have been omitted: the development of a written strategic plan and a content strategy.

Based on years of experience and speaking with hundreds of professionals who have forayed into the wilds of social media, I find feelings and conclusions that social media is a waste of time, effort and finance. But, listen to me, please: anything conducted *incorrectly* is going to flop. Build an airplane incorrectly and it will crash, if it ever gets up into the air in the first place.

Does this mean that flying is an outmoded form of transportation? Of course not.

While by no means does this following list represent all one should learn about, or everything one can do concerning, social media marketing, here are some quick tips offered on how to go about social media marketing more effectively:

- Begin by developing a simple marketing strategy.
- Know what you want to say to what audience(s) that you want to reach and convert.
- Have a marketing budget in mind that will be workable.
- Begin with a blog and/or video as your prime source(s) of newly created content.
- Check over the various types of content that could be created and list out two or three additional types of content that you could create while remaining within your resources and budget.
- Determine what distribution channels you can leverage to best reach your target audience; focus on those first.
- Automate the delivery of your social media posts with Hootsuite, Klout or another similar platform.
- Ensure that all your social profiles are secured and branded correctly, so that your audience clearly knows that it is you.
- See if paid ads on social channels are a worthwhile investment; engage if they are within your budget.
- Involve your employees in sharing your content, even in helping your content creation with their perspectives or shared information about how clients are enjoying (or not) your products/services.
- Figure out how you can get your customers involved as "brand advocates" that will share your products and services via their social channels to their followers. Get creative with them, but respectfully.

- Develop a formal strategy to get your customers to create and/or contribute content, including online reviews, videos, photos on Instagram, or even guest-blog postings.
- Rapidly figure out how to incorporate more video as a prime piece of content shared on your social channels.

How to Get More Followers

Building an audience is one of the biggest challenges about using social media. The way to fast track this is with paid ads or sponsored posts offered by several social channels.

Unfortunately, the average small business owner, entrepreneur or startup has no extra money to spend on advertising in order to build new followers. Here, however, are some tips on how to grow followers with *zero financial investment*:

- Concentrate on the one or two social platforms that make the most sense for your brand and audience. Versus trying to be everywhere, you want to "fish where the fish are." Facebook is best for B2C, and LinkedIn is where B2B resides. Instagram is a must if you want to reach Millennials, while Pinterest is great for married and divorced women. Twitter is excellent for reaching high-tech companies, bloggers, media and entertainment-related services and publications.
- Once you determine the one or two social channels you plan to concentrate on, read books and blogs about that specific social channel. Though I am offering some very quick tips – a brief overview, really – more in-depth study should be an activity you do pursue to become proficient with social media. Plenty of experts on YouTube will share with you tremendous

insights for each and every social channel. One of the keys to competence is to be an eternal student.

* Utilize Hashtagify.me to find out what the hashtags trends are for your brand. Share content with the right hashtags. As well, see what hashtags your competitors are using that are getting likes and shares. Emulate those social media success cases.

* Many social channels offer "suggested people" to follow. Look these over and send an invite or a connection to those who align with your branding efforts. (Send invites to business owners, CEOs, doctors, bloggers and leaders in social media. Once they connect, I usually send a note of thanks.)

* Post great content daily. I suggest 60 percent curated content and 40 percent your own material. Curated content from articles, industry news, inspirational quotes and interesting facts, makes for good posts.

* Participate! This is SOCIAL media, so be social and comment on the posts of others. Reach out and be an active member within your community of followers.

* Use social media automation tools to make your postings easier and more efficient to produce and distribute. Check out Hootsuite, SocialOomph, Dlvt.it, Buffer and Klout to find which one you prefer.

There is so much to learn about social media, and, in fact, many books and hundreds of blogs are published almost daily that can help you.

My effort here is only to help you to delineate what social media is and how to go about engaging with it effectively and rapidly. Seek consulting as you see fit and keep your own counsel. Make your own decisions; whatever seems right for you.

Every feature of every (new and old) social media platform should be perused and considered a part of your social branding, social business, or social-selling strategic plan.

The "old saw" applies: *"Plan your work, and work your plan."* And persist. Be flexible and willing to tweak and alter what does not work until you find what is the right combination(s) for you.

BRANDING, IMAGES AND SOCIAL MEDIA

Images are an important aspect of branding on social media. The way logos, fonts, point sizes, and colors work together in social media is an important aspect for you to consider about gaining brand recognition.

Consistency is a big factor. Ensure that are your social channels have the brand's logo custom fit and sized for each social channel's design and size specifications. Ensure that watermarks or logos appear on all photos, memes and infographics.

Created, beautiful designs, photos, artwork and layouts play a big role in standing out and ensuring that your brand's image makes a continuous, positive, memorable impression in your audiences' minds. More than two billion people active on social media pages and channels every day, make your visual assets important factors that can keep your brand awareness at the top of minds and ahead of your competitors.

CHAPTER 23
Native Advertising

As your brand and your budget grow, native advertising becomes a potent method for your *Power Brand* to reach and engage a larger audience.

> "Native advertising is an online advertising method in which the advertiser attempts to gain attention by providing content in the context of the user's experience. Native ad formats match both the form and the function of the user experience in which it is placed. The advertiser's intent is to make the paid advertising feel less intrusive and thus increase the likelihood users will click on it." – Wikipedia

Simply explained, native advertising is paid-content marketing that couples editorial standards to the target audience's expectations. When an ad is more about information than direct selling, and it aligns to the visual standards of a publication inviting readers to engage with it, you have an example of native advertising.

Power Brand marketers know that their best-written, best designed content fulfills its purpose best in native ads, advertorial strategies and tactics. To qualify, the content must behave consistently and contextually within the native user's experience and expectations, and it must function like natural content.

As Reuters columnist Felix Salmon noted, "A native ad is something that consumers read, interact with, even share — it fills up their attention space, for a certain period of time, in a way that banner ads never do... In that sense, TV ads are truly native; the way you consume a TV ad is the same as the way you consume a TV show. Similarly, long-copy print ads are native, for the same reason. And the ultimate native ads are the glossy fashion ads in Vogue: In most cases, they're better than the editorial, and as a result, readers spend as much time with the ads — if not more — as they do with the edit."

HISTORICAL EXAMPLES OF NATIVE ADVERTISING

Native advertising has been around with us for a while, even though it was not referred to as such. Here are some historical examples of native advertising methods and campaigns:

- 1776: Thomas Paine wrote the pamphlet, *Common Sense,* which became an immediate sensation at the beginning of the American Revolution. It was sold and distributed widely and read aloud at taverns and common meeting places. General George Washington had it read to all of his troops before making his famous crossing of the Delaware River, which resulted in surrounding a surprised the British army at Trenton, New Jersey. (The tactic broke the back of the Redcoats offensive assault on the emerging nation.) In proportion to the population of the colonies at that time (2.5 million), Paine's publication had the largest sale and circulation in American history.

- In 1891, August Oetker sold small packages of his *Backin* baking powder to households with recipes printed on the back. In 1911, he published the first edition of his very successful cookbook, which has gone through major updates over the past 100 years and is one of the most successful cookbooks globally, reaching 19 million printed copies to date. All of the recipes originated from the test kitchen of the Oetker Company. The book was carefully written as a textbook to teach readers how to cook from scratch.

* In 1895, John Deere launched the magazine *The Furrow,* providing information to farmers on how to become more profitable. Considered the first custom publication, the magazine is still in circulation with a reach to 1.5 million readers in 40 countries in 12 different languages.

* In 1900, Michelin developed the *Michelin Guide,* offering driver's information on auto maintenance, accommodations, and other travel tips. 35,000 copies were distributed for free in this first edition. Although Michelin eventually began selling these books, the publication had set a precedent for both informative guides and content marketing distribution.

* In 1904, Jell-O salesmen went door-to-door, distributing their product-related cookbook for free. Touting the dessert as a versatile food, the company saw its sales rise to over $1 million by 1906.

NATIVE ADVERTISING AND YOU

So, how can this new term and activity, *native advertising,* be put to work for your **Power Brand**? You need to develop ads, videos, booklets, and other content that is more information- and news-driven than a sales-driven approach with a call to action of a purchase. These can include "how to" information pamphlets, guidebooks, courses, cookbooks, and other practical collections of information designed to inform, teach or fill in the gaps of missing data.

Here are some examples of how to *implement* native advertising as a small business:

- A small café can create a series of videos on how to create some of their most requested coffees.
- A local restaurant could create a guidebook, printed as well as an eBook, of their popular recipes, as well as tips on how to select the best and freshest ingredients for home-cooking use.
- Twitter should create a free online course, "Neat Tweets." Too many people who begin with Twitter last less than seven days.
- A mechanic could put out a guidebook on how to fix common problems with cars — changing oil and other fluids, etc. — as well as replacing old wiper blades. These could be placed prominently in auto parts stores, dry cleaners, etc., and made accessible as a PDF download from their website.
- A men's suits store could publish an in-store pamphlet, as well as a downloadable PDF, that shares data about the various methods of how to tie a tie.
- Paid ads written as articles also could be placed on local and/or niche blogs, ensuring attribution as sponsored content.

Even though most businesses and their brands struggle to implement native advertising creatively and successfully, this type of advertising remains an important branding and marketing strategy for generating positive attention, new sales and more customers.

While native advertising, at first glance, may appear to be out of reach for some small businesses and startups, they should not negate the opportunity to leverage its content to feature their brand as a ***Power Brand.***

CHAPTER 24

Marketing Automation

❖ ❖ ❖

SOONER OR LATER, ONCE YOU begin to consistently create and distribute your branded content to your target audiences, you will have to manage your time and resources more efficiently with automation.

> "Marketing automation refers to software platforms and technologies designed for marketing departments and organizations to more effectively market on multiple channels online (such as email, social media, websites, etc.) and automate repetitive tasks. Marketing departments, consultants and part-time marketing employees benefit by specifying criteria and outcomes for tasks and processes which are then interpreted, stored and executed by software, which increases efficiency and reduces human error. Originally focused on email marketing automation, marketing automation refers to a broad range of automation and analytic tools for marketing especially inbound marketing. Marketing Automation platforms are used as a hosted or web-based solution, and no software installation is required by a customer. The use of a marketing automation platform is to streamline sales and marketing organizations by replacing high-touch, repetitive manual processes with automated solutions." - Wikipedia

In short, marketing automation uses software and tactics that allow companies to market to and nurture prospects with highly personalized, useful content, while saving time and human resources. Marketing automation typically generates a much higher level of new revenue for companies and provides an excellent ROI for the expenditure from one's marketing budget.

Truth be told, initial use of automated marketing can be quite complex, yet not impossible to learn. Imagine you're trying to grow a plant. At first, you need fertile soil. Next, you need seeds, and lastly you need water and light to nurture those seeds into lush, blooming plants—the method is not foolproof, but not impossible, either. Effective marketing automation works just like nurturing these plants: at the end of the day, we hope our leads (seedlings) produce actual paying customers. (lush, full-grown plants.)

KEEPING ONE'S EXPECTATIONS REAL

In the last few years, "marketing automation" has become an industry-wide buzz-word. Unfortunately, many marketers got caught up in the hyperbole surrounding its introduction and they embraced marketing-automation software under the impression that it was the only digital-marketing tool necessary for customer-base growth, expecting it to generate new leads automatically. This misconception carried forward, leaving those and other marketers with sophisticated tools to automate the middle of their sales funnel, but no solution to generate new leads to nurture in the first place.

The result? Brand marketing teams began to purchase large lists of email addresses versus work to generate their own inbound, hot-prospect leads. The false impression left by automated marketing made it appear to be an easy-to-apply, quick fix for an ongoing problem. In actual practice, automated marketing is neither a long-term, leads-generation solution, nor fertile ground for nurturing genuine and highly sustainable relationships with a company's clientele.

Any farmer worth the fruits of his labors knows that using artificial chemicals to make crops grow faster, in the long run, will bring the yield, and eventually entire fields, to ruin.

Automated marketing should occupy a definite space within your strategic-marketing plans and tactics, but by no means does it represent everything you should be doing to create and distribute content to your inbound leads and overall clientele.

AUTOMATED MARKETING'S EXPLODING GROWTH

Raab Associates, Inc., a 21-year old, respected consultancy, expected marketing automation to grow by 60% in 2014 and to generate $1.2 billion in sales. The continued rise in revenue indicates an increased sophistication in the B2B market, forcing content marketers to be more strategic for their organizations.

On the other hand, there are additional statistics that reveal that automated marketing does not equate to automatic success. According to Sirius Decisions, a leading global B2B research and advisory firm, a whopping 75 percent of those entities in possession of and using marketing automation complain that they are not getting the full value from it.

Where lies the correct solutions to the chasm between promise and profitability?

As more organizations make investments into marketing automation software, the door remains wide open for plenty of mistakes to be made. A recent Forrester study showed that of 25 different tactics listed, B2B organizations are using on average only 15 different tactics in their demand/generation mix. A similar question posed to respondents by Content Marketing Institute showed 13 was the average.

Here, then, are some quick tips on how to avoid common pitfalls, as well as generate a successful model of activities attractive to your best long-term clientele:

- Develop a strategic plan that coordinates all channels for content creation and distribution. A comprehensive strategy ensures that all your efforts across multiple platforms, systems and team members, dovetail into a seamless, holistic effort.
- To improve the quality of returns from your automation expenditure, you to need to ensure that you are training personnel for maximized content output, distribution and placement, as well as measurement and understanding of those returns. (Side note: After purchasing expensive and complex software, most companies are lax in their planning and estimation of how much initial education and continuing education will be required to maximize their software's capabilities.)
- Create quality content. This begins with market research that truly uncovers what your target audiences think, feel and desire. Research into what types of content your audience(s) consume(s), and from what media channels, is necessary. Are they more video oriented, or reading longer, more detailed, written reports and studies?
- Set realistic targets and measure those consistently. Adjust your efforts based on the numbers that are coming back to you on a weekly or monthly basis. As well, implement A/B (two variants) testing with all of your automated marketing so that you can examine what changes in design, copy and distribution are generating more user traffic and purchases.

CALLS TO ACTION

When all is said and done, the ultimate goal of all branding, marketing, content creation and distribution is the earned business of a customer for a company's products and services.

"A call to action, or CTA, is a banner, button, or some type of graphic or text on a website meant to prompt a user to click it and continue down a conversion funnel." - Wikipedia

Often Marketing's biggest challenges are the long sales cycles and complex decision-making processes that prospects and existing customers go through to decide to make a purchase. Increasing pressure on marketing professionals exists to find the most qualified prospects and build relationships with them before the lead is passed to Sales. This is the reason why Marketing needs to develop germane, effective calls to action attached to all of its offers, emails and content.

Here are some CTA tips, which can be worked into your creative content and your automated marketing campaigns:

* Add clearly visible buttons for people to click. Embedded within these buttons, add phrases like, "Start Free Now" or "Sign Up Here."
* Ensure that your call-to-action buttons are large enough, are tastefully designed, have contrasting colors, are easy to find, and look like buttons.
* Prominently position the buttons in a distinguishable place that naturally follows the flow of copy and design of the page.
* Offer a choice as a potential call to action. Give two options as a call to action versus taking an action or not.
* Boost your buttons with "click trigger" copy. Examples: you can write above your button, triggers such as testimonials, payback guarantees, easy-payment options, star ratings, and more.

Drip-Marketing Campaigns

To generate healthy and steady business from your target audiences, nurture your prospects; do not overwhelm them with too much content or requests for purchase. Not only is this common sense, but also a requisite. To not do so will leave you with less followers, more email opt-outs and, worse, a damaged brand with negative word of mouth and online reviews that will cause further damage. So just do not push too hard, too soon or too often.

Drip marketing can be a highly effective marketing technique that spoon-feeds great content over time, rather than an obnoxious tsunami of unwanted, unread, interruptive advertising.

"Drip marketing is a communication strategy that sends, or 'drips,' a pre-written set of messages to customers or prospects over time. These messages often take the form of email marketing, although other media can also be used. Drip marketing is distinct from other database marketing in two ways: (1) the timing of the messages follow a pre-determined course; (2) the messages are dripped in a series applicable to a specific behavior or status of the recipient. It is also typically automated." - Wikipedia

Although drip marketing has been conducted with direct mail and with social media, the most common practice of drip marketing is with email. Drip marketing helps companies to generate leads and to move these leads through a qualification process.

In actual usage in the content marketing world, drip marketing is automated follow-up capable of enhancing or even fully replacing sales lead follow-ups from live personnel. The use of Autoresponders is quite common in conjunction with automated marketing and the resultant drip-marketing campaign. As new visitors enter the email address, a pre-programmed drip marketing campaign begins automatically with messaging relevant to the call to action from which the lead came. This process is often referred as lead nurturing.

The advantages to **Power Brand** marketers with this type of automation are abundantly clear:

* Incredible efficiency added to one's marketing efforts.
* 24/7 ability for direct response.
* Brand ability to consistently reach audiences over a longer period of time.
* Trust building with your audience.

But, there are definite *disadvantages* to this type of marketing, not the least of which is the impersonal manner of how the follow-up is conducted. Sales conversion rates may also suffer. Still, many companies can justify the lowered response rate by the sheer capability of volume outreach combined with an increase in efficiency with which leads can be generated and converted.

I do suggest that you work with automated marketing solutions – AWeber and Infusionsoft are two providers of the service – as a means to nurture more leads, using an efficient and effective marketing model.

CHAPTER 25

Power Branding and Public Relations

"If I was down to my last dollar, I would spend it on public relations." – Bill Gates

PUBLIC RELATIONS (PR) IS BETTER than advertising for building a brand, argued Laura and Al Ries in their prophetic 2002 book, *The Fall of Advertising and the Rise of PR*. At the time, they were right; advertising had indeed lost credibility whereas other media still had it.

Media is constantly pressured to compromise its impartiality. For one thing, there now exists a constant need to produce news 24 hours a day, seven days a week. Additionally, the media are owned by mega-sized corporate entities in business primarily to generate profits: the press survives by selling airtime and print space to advertisers.

These two factors together, in addition to any internal bias from a media entity itself, leaves media vulnerable to press releases and prepackaged content put together by private agencies hoping to get the word out about their clients, especially if those clients are willing to underwrite advertising time and space.

However, the viewing or listening public is aware; people are not stupid. When a television segment on health is sponsored by the same entity featured in an aired story, the media platform which aired it loses credibility.

I would argue that the role of PR was never to build a brand in the first place. Rather, PR's role for a ***Power Brand*** is to repair harm done to it, to prevent harm from occurring, and, inherently, to build great reputations. Moreover, great PR will ignite a fire of buzz, allowing marketing to reap more rewards from a clamorous and interested audience.

As **PRinfluences.au** writes, "A strong corporate reputation is increasingly a PR responsibility. Image can... be generated through an advertising campaign or a corporate document or the look of an organization's premises... [while] reputation is... built through developing relationships and what an organization does. It is largely what others say about you."

One implication is that PR grows the reputation to protect the brand. Just to clarify: Reputation—which can loosely be defined as trustworthiness—is not the totality of the brand. Branding manages *image*, while reputation, PR's domain, concentrates on *reality*.

What this means is that branding is prone to fakery, whereas reputation is much closer to reality. Branding, therefore, is best conveyed by a consistent sales/marketing/advertising "core message," while reputation is best conveyed by transparency. Both need execution to complete a ***Power Brand*** experience.

In other words, Branding relates to Image; PR relates to reputation or reality.

"It takes 20 years to build a reputation and five minutes to ruin it. If you think about that, you'll do things differently." – Warren Buffet

THE POWER OF BUZZ

PR creates word-of-mouth opportunities like no other type of brand-building activity. Public Relations proactively develops traction with the media, key leaders, influential bloggers, industry writers and target audiences through media contacts, events, one-on-one contact and well-crafted press releases. Creating a positive buzz through such actions generates credibility and respect for your *Power Brand.*

Other successful PR activities include having the CEO to speak in favor of causes the *Power Brand* supports; be active with community-based activities, and in general enable PR to create content that is primarily produced to showcase newsworthy activities and accomplishments.

Consumers have become somewhat weary of brands and their promises due to the fact that too many of them have come up short on delivering. Just know that consumers are going to dig around concerning your brand to see what others are saying about you. They want to rate your "buzz factor" and genuineness from other consumers, the media and bloggers. A *Power Brand* must take control of their PR and thus build positive, genuine buzz as a part of their branding and marketing strategy.

BUILDING RELATIONSHIPS: THE MEDIA AND THE CITIZEN REPORTER

In today's world, the word *Media* represents a larger force than the circle of reporters hobnobbing at the press club of the old days. From a publication or news agency, today's "reporters" are just as likely, if not more so, to be influential bloggers and social media influencers (Think *The Matt Drudge Report.*), which can shape perception of your ***Power Brand*** just as effectively as the remaining, traditional media giants.

Still, it is important that you develop relationships with all of them: agencies, bloggers and other social media influencers that have the attention of your target audience. For a local business, this may be local bloggers and local newspapers and publications. For a CPA, this could mean business journals and specific, financial-related bloggers, who write about tax law and accounting software.

FEED THEM WHAT THEY WANT

These agencies and individuals are looking for news, novel ideas, innovations, and accomplishments worth talking about and sharing. Ask yourself: If I were an industry writer, reporter, editor or local blogger, what would I want to write about? What do I see that my audience would find of interest?

See the connection? You need to start thinking like a reporter to get your point across to these media hounds and to your audiences. Approach them from a newsworthy perspective, not from a marketing angle.

When your brand is featured helping people, shaping new innovations, or having accomplished something notable, others in the media brigade will advocate for your story and your existence, not to mention your acumen and prowess. In turn, you share these aired news features on your website, on social channels, in your emails and your sales decks.

"As seen in/on_____.," lends credibility and can lead to further positive press coverage.

If you can afford the expense, hire someone as an employee (part-time or full-time), or an outside PR agency, to contact selected media outlets and bloggers, establish rapport with them, and then discover from them the type of news that they deem worthy of featuring. Stories can then be created and shared with the hope that they will be aired by the media to their followers or subscribers.

TRANSPARENCY AND PR

Transparency — the real job of a PR professional (though they may not be able to openly express it in practice), tells the whole, acceptable truth and nothing but the truth about the organization; in so doing it portrays the organization as trustworthy. PR, in fact, is the other side of the coin of branding, which, by itself, is tasked to tell a truth favoring the better side of the brand. Really, branding is pure marketing. Branding takes aim at portraying and then owning a single idea in the audience's mind. No matter how they are written up in *The Wall Street Journal* or *Fortune*, the brands of BMW, Nike, Disney, Starbucks, and Pepsi, to name only a few, have little to do with the real-world activities inside of their organizations, and much more to do with the image they project to the public.

"Without publicity there can be no public support, and without public support every nation must decay." – Benjamin Disraeli

There is one exception, and that is where PR and transparency combines for a specific purpose. As mentioned above, PR leverages transparency to build up the reputation of a brand and to safeguard its image against damaging attacks. So, when Starbucks embarks on a PR-driven, corporate/citizenship, interactive campaign like "fair-trade coffee beans," the intended effect is not to build or enhance the brand's sales, but rather to enhance the company's reputation. Once again, reputation is the domain of PR.

Let's face it: Starbucks doesn't get $2-plus for a cup of coffee because of its coffee bean policy but because Starbucks represents something completely different and special in the minds of its consumers: "time out for myself."

The Starbucks *brand* is the product of all the activities it undertakes to promote its image; speaking about its reality, the number of sold cups of coffee is the bottom line. When Starbucks' television commercials show frenzied mothers taking time out for a Frappuccino, or a young worker rushing to get to the office but taking time out for a refrigerated Starbucks DoubleShot Espresso, image (brand) is king... but only to propel the flow of coffee and dollars-exchanged.

The only reason for reputation-building activities, or PR, is to protect the brand against being damaged by scandal or rumors. Thus far, we have established that PR does not build the brand, but rather defends and elevates the brand's reputation. But one can go even further than this.

To harken back to the initial discussion of Media's tarnished objectivity: today's PR has a new hurdle to face in defending a company's reputation, and that is to actually deliver transparency. It is no longer sufficient for PR to develop and disseminate truths delivered with a credible source, but emphasizing only the positive.

Rather, to counter the perceived bias of the media, PR has to deliver objective information about an organization to the media, even when that information sounds or appears negative. Otherwise, jaded viewers will know that the media has been corrupted by a "PR" message, and they will simply tune out.

"Publicity is absolutely critical. A good PR story is infinitely more effective than a front-page ad." – Sir Richard Branson

NETWORKING IN PERSON

An important element in power branding and public relations is the proactive IRL (In Real Life) spokesperson for your brand. The impact of networking in person cannot be overstated; this includes your willingness to get involved in public-speaking opportunities to groups, both small and large.

Personal networking makes for deeper relationships, greater co-operation and more progress toward your branding and marketing goals. Yet, too often it becomes an overlooked branding and marketing factor in our fast-paced digital age.

I have garnered many speaking opportunities by including "keynote speaker" in my profile on LinkedIn, Twitter and other social media profiles. I will also occasionally post on my networks that I am available to speak. Without question, public speakers are viewed as experts and authorities in their respective fields, like published authors.

An additional benefit of networking in person and public speaking is that these keep you in touch with the jugulars of new trends; buzz words that are cropping up; new topics of interest; and other bits of relevant information that keep you tuned to what is news in the world and in your field of endeavor or business.

Place yourself on the live, electric lines of the real world — often. Attend industry events, workshops, seminars and parties. Each face-to-face performance and communication will pack a bigger punch for your brand than any Facebook chat or Twitter conversation ever will. The important point is to be where business is occurring, where collaboration is taking place and, in real time, make yourself a vibrant participant.

PUBLIC RELATIONS IS MORE IMPORTANT THAN EVER

"Public relations is booming at present, and its mechanisms and practices are being adopted by corporations and companies across the globe. Journalism in the developed world is undergoing a series of radical changes, and is available in a greater choice of forms than ever before." - John Lloyd and Laura Toogood, co-authors of *Journalism and PR*

With radical changes come amazing opportunities for a ***Power Brand*** that comprehends that PR can be a key difference in how the brand is perceived and a valued.

PR is no longer just about corporate messaging. It's about conversation. PR isn't blasting noise and information – it's creating sustainable stories and leveraging new digital tools to give them life. PR is about creating innovative ways to connect a ***Power Brand*** with its audience in an authentic manner.

CHAPTER 26

Distribution is Half the Work

WHILE CREATING BRANDED CONTENT CAN consume much time in the ideation, imagery, design, and development of your brand image and company ethos, half of your time, efforts and expenses should be expended on the *distribution* of your branded content.

If "Content is king," as the famous saying goes, distribution is the ruling queen, and, like chess, the queen owns the big moves. Without appearing when and where people require or seek information, your content is useless.

Lacking a promotional distribution strategy, most of your branded content will continue to flounder and go unread. To be relevant, your branded content must be seen, consumed, shared and eventually impel its readers to conduct business with your brand. Therefore, a distribution strategy to build up your followers on social media, add more email addresses to your list, and increase your face-to-face engagements with consumers at webinars, workshops, conferences, and other events, is vital to your branded content's viability and the success of your business.

THREE TYPES OF STRATEGIC MEDIA DISTRIBUTION
Before we dive into the tools, let's start with an overview of content distribution. Essentially, when you distribute your content, you do so through three basic channels.

1. **Owned**
2. **Earned**
3. **Paid**

Owned media includes the channels that belong to you, where you control the content. These include your mailing list, blog, website, emailed newsletter, and social media profiles.

Shared content created by you is **Earned Media,** which includes social-media shares, retweets, customer reviews, media coverage, and industry-related articles.

Paid media is the exposure you pay for, such as paid ads in print, radio and television media. It would also encompass distributed fliers and handouts.

There are other means of reaching a broader spectrum of audiences; some are free and some are paid-distribution channels.

- **Social Bookmarking** - A social bookmarking service is a centralized online service that enables users to add, annotate, edit, and share bookmarks of web documents. Sites like Stumbleupon have paid-distribution options, as well as capability and space for posting your content on their site for free. Other popular social bookmarking sites are Reddit, Digg and Del.icio.us.
- **Press releases** - Writing and publishing press releases is an effective pattern for (with a long-standing history of success) distributing news that attracts attention. Services such as PR Newswire, PR Web and the cost-effective option I have used with success, 24-7 Press Release. (See this book's section on how to generate positive media for your power branding.)
- **Guest Posting** - Guest posting or republishing existing content on other blogs is one of the best ways to generate initial

traffic for your blog. By writing on another's blog, you reach dedicated audiences, which trusted others have built up with loyal followers. A great resource for finding other bloggers is InkyBee.com.

- **LinkedIn Influencer** - In 2013, LinkedIn announced their Influencer platform to the public. From it, any LinkedIn member can self-publish, syndicate, and distribute content on LinkedIn's robust platform. What's important to keep in mind about LinkedIn's platform is that it centers on individuals, not their brand. In other words, LinkedIn is not brand-centric. This is one channel on which it is important to post as an individual, rather than a representative of a brand. This platform allows many individuals connected with one brand to create multiple business-related snippets of brand content, thus attracting more attention to (those who work for) the brand. The key to succeeding on LinkedIn is to add value and insight. To date, I have personally leveraged this platform to publish over 75 articles.

- **Outbrain.com** - Outbrain is a lot like Google Adwords regarding content. Publishers provide an RSS feed of their content or submit individual links, and Outbrain produces headlines at the bottom of stories posted on major media sites under the labels, "Sponsored" or "Related."

- **Zemanta.com** - Zemanta is a link distribution engine cleverly disguised as a text editor plugin. The consumer-facing side of Zemanta's software analyzes the content of blog posts in progress and suggests relevant photos and links for authors to add on the fly.

- **Oneload.com** - Social media expert Gary Vaynerchuk plugs this site relentlessly in his book *Crush It*. In short, OneLoad allows users to upload a video once, and then automatically distribute it across a wide network of popular social and video networks.

- **Paid Advertising on Social Media** - Facebook, Twitter and LinkedIn have robust paid programs to reach highly targeted audiences. Before you spend any money on this, however, I suggest that you contact a digital-media agency with experience using this type of content distribution. The best method is to advertise free-item-offer pages, such as a free white paper or an ecourse, in return for harvested emails, to which you can further market. Paid social media can drive consumers to your content, attract new subscribers, and further market your brand.

- **Employee Advocacy** - One of the largest, missed, branding and marketing opportunities for brands is getting their employees to share the company's branded content to their social media contacts. Even a small cafe may have up to 20 different employees working various shifts throughout a week. Most of these employees likely have followers on Facebook, Instagram, Vine, Snapchat and Twitter. This example alone would represent a combined, potential audience of over 20,000 coffee drinkers just from the employees' networks! I would suggest that you survey to find out what type of content they would like the brand to publish, and if respondees would be willing to create content that others can share. You are tapping into the collective creativity and genius, and contacts, of your employees is a smart idea.

- **Consumer-Generated Content** - Just as employee engagement is vital, your consumer base represents another, larger base of content distributors capable of online reviews. Multiple studies and surveys have shown that consumer-generated content is *the most preferred and trusted content, more than any advertising you could pay for.* This is why online reviews on Amazon drive sales and rankings, and why Yelp reviews are coveted like marketing gold. Any knowledgeable small business owner will tell you that online reviews can make or break their business. The

Power Brand Doritos, for instance, encourages contests whereby people create videos showing why they love their Doritos chips. Thousands of people participate, sharing their love for their brand to their social media contacts and in the process making the Doritos brand strategically acceptable and more popular.

* **Strategic Alliances** - Also known as joint venture or partnership marketing. The most cost-effective marketing known to the gods of branding is to combine forces with other brands. When your brand shares the spotlight with a brand that is already trusted, trust is transferred to your brand. If the other brand is larger and more established than yours, their *Power Brand status is practically transferred to your brand by the association.* For small businesses and startups, this represents a workable, and envied, branding strategy.

    For example: a new real estate agent could team up with established interior decorators, local moving companies, or even divorce lawyers. Someone purchasing from an established brand more than likely will be open to looking at other brands that compliment theirs. So, why not take those natural "brand search" efforts and develop them into strategic alliances with respected, established brands?

* **Help Out a Reporter (HARO)** - HelpAReporter.com lets you connect with journalists looking for a source. If you've got an expertise or experience in a certain area, you can sign up at HARO and a reporter might get in touch with you... might even air or print your opinion or information!

EMAIL MARKETING

For its cost and ROI potential, nothing beats email for your branding and marketing efforts. While much talk and buzz about social media and how to harness its venues continues, when you look at the hard numbers of email's sheer size and prowess, and its ROI, business marketing by email has to be considered the backbone of your marketing strategy.

Did you know that email has nearly *three times* as many user accounts as Facebook and Twitter *combined?* That's a whopping 2.9 billion. In fact, Facebook and Twitter combined make up just 0.2 percent of the number of emails sent each day.

For small business owners email is the inexpensive and most-effective method of choice to establish or maintain relationships with clientele. But, there is a catch: email content has the power to either attract or repel. Before you hit "send" on your next batch of email newsletters, take care, and spend time considering the content of what you are about to send.

Marketers and non-marketers alike share a mutual concern for doing email marketing the right way: are the emails they're sending making it into the inboxes and pleasing their recipients; wasted by filters and dumped into spam files; or, worse, annoyances of their targeted audiences?

The truly curious marketers constantly wonder about and work to improve the response rates of their email campaigns.

But, let's look at email's other advantages as a marketing tool. By survey,

1. Most consumers find email easier to access for information than most social-media platforms.
2. Email is much more transactional versus social. 65 percent of Americans will purchase something in the next 6 months as a result of an email. Social media does not even come close to driving sales like email.

3. Email is 40 years old and as such is a grooved-in, verified, commercial platform. Consumers and marketers alike understand it, while for most people, social media still feels like that "new-fangled thing."

EMAIL PROVIDERS

Many reputable and effective email-marketing companies offer templates and automated-response systems to help you design and distribute professional emails.

I find those that provide help through simple tips are best.

What is really great about these email providers is that they provide a ton of resources regarding how to conduct your email campaigns the right way. I could go into the details of each, but my best advice is to find one that you like, learn their system and start sending out your own weekly emails of helpful tips, articles, your latest blog posts, and your new offerings.

BEST METHODS TO DISTRIBUTE BRANDED CONTENT

Today, the scarcest resource in the brand-marketing field is not branded content, but the audience that is receiving and consuming your branded content. To compete for readership attention, brands and content creators find they not only have to produce better content, but also effective strategies and channels in which to place that content in front of people.

Fortunately, tools are emerging to help those engaged in marketing to reach new audiences, but getting more readers won't be much help if your content is terrible or even mediocre. With distribution tools like those listed below, content marketers can worry less about reach and more about producing quality content. The key fundamental regarding your content distribution is to create great content that people will *want* to engage with and share. As you begin to consistently create engaging and worthwhile content, the distribution methods you choose will support its growth.

- Search engines (Content must be SEO robust.)
- Email
- RSS/Syndication
- Twitter
- Facebook
- LinkedIn
- Google+
- YouTube
- Pinterest
- Instagram
- Tumblr
- Slideshare
- Direct Mail
- Webinars
- Live streaming
- Live seminars and workshops
- Tradeshows
- iTunes (podcasts and music)
- Discussion forums
- Reddit
- Digg
- Delicious
- Stumbleupon
- Influencers & strategic partnerships
- Guest blogging
- Industry specific conferences

- Paid advertising & distribution
- Blogging communities
- Press release agencies and syndicates
- Press conferences
- Sales team members and employees
- Newsletters (e-version and printed)
- Widgets & Apps
- Radio & TV interviews and shows
- Printed materials, such as business cards & brochures
- Annual reports
- Signage

CHAPTER 27

Branding & Our Real-time World

YOU SHOULD ATTEMPT TO ESTABLISH your *Power Brand* by publishing content and news as closely as possible to real-time. If you're not engaged at the speed of business, you're on your way out, no longer relevant to the marketplace.

Real-time is news that breaks over minutes, not days. Real-time does not wait for monthly or quarterly planning sessions. It means ideas that percolate among small groups of individuals and then, suddenly and unpredictably, they go viral across the global stage.

Power Brands, to establish relevancy with larger audiences, need to develop or reconfigure their branding and marketing strategies, as Don Henley sang it, "In a New York Minute." They need to listen attentively to feedback from customers, industry leaders, and even their competitors.

Power Brands must seize upon real-time opportunities and be the first to act on them successfully. Going viral is the Holy Grail of brand marketing online.

"Scale and media-buying power are no longer a decisive advantage. What counts today is speed and agility." - David Meerman Scott

Companies still incapacitated with a pre-internet mindset and time-consuming business processes, miss online opportunities. These (failure-bound) companies expose themselves fatally to irrelevancy and knockout punches from competitors by flying blind through to-day's digital-media environment. Fortunately, their numbers are going down. In fact, 76 percent of executives surveyed by Evergage use real-time marketing (RTM), and 40 percent of CMOs surveyed by Accenture believe RTM campaigns are the future of marketing.

In a February 2014 survey by Evergage, fielded by Researchscape International, around three-quarters of surveyed marketing professionals worldwide defined RTM as personalizing content in response to consumer interactions. This makes sense, because greater than eight out of 10 marketers cited increasing customer engagement as a benefit of RTM's personalized, targeted interactions.

EXAMPLES OF RTM
Good RTM content adds value, whether by pure entertainment or delivery of something consumers want at the time they want it.

The Emmy-awards ceremony events interest viewers interested to see what celebrities are wearing *right now* while the Emmys are live. Recently, on seeing and hearing the buzz surrounding Tina Fey's dress, Target showed their customers how they could get a similar look within their (demographic) price range—and that's exactly what Target fans wanted to know at that moment.

When singer Pharell Williams showed up at the 2014 Grammys wearing a hat that resembled the Arby's logo, the restaurant chain playfully tweeted "Hey @Pharell, can we have our hat back? #GRAMMYs." Tweeters following the Grammys hashtag, and others, likely saw that tweet in their feed. In fact, it was retweeted over 81,000 times! Several months later, Pharell auctioned off the hat on eBay and raised funds for a charity helping at-risk kids. Guess who bought the Arby's logo-replica hat for over $41,000.

That's right: Arby's!

Real-time Marketing at its finest.

In the future, more than half of strategic-plan management of a social campaign may take place *after* a campaign starts, estimates Colin Mitchell, Worldwide Head of Planning at Ogilvy & Mather. In a white paper by Mitchell, he stressed the importance of dynamic content, conversation management, and nurtured, real-time optimization within modern-day marketing campaigns. He also identified six new skills to navigate these new waters:

1. Planning for talk – Brands need to know their point of view and be prepared to engage, if they want to be the topic of conversation.
2. Rapid-response research – Listening will become a core practice; research will have to be about the here and now.
3. Rapid prototyping – The days of having months or years to perfect a campaign are long over.
4. Opportunistic media – Media partners of the future will collaborate more effectively with agencies for media placement.
5. Plan for the end – A story has a beginning, a middle and an end. Don't fade away; give your audience a satisfying ending.
6. Spread the payments – This applies to in-house marketers as much as agencies. Understand that a budget needs to extend across the life of a campaign and that the bulk of that effort is shifting from preparation to management.

Newsjacking and Branded Content

If you have ever leveraged a real-time opportunity by writing a blog post, launching a social media campaign, getting press coverage or video commentary on YouTube in an effort to attract more attention and followers to your brand, then you have practiced Newsjacking.

Newsjacking refers to the practice of capitalizing on the popularity of a news story to amplify your own brand awareness and marketing initiatives. The term was popularized through David Meerman Scott's book, *Newsjacking: How to Inject Your Ideas into a Breaking News Story and Generate Tons of Media Coverage.* The basic tenet and practice goes like this: whenever news is breaking every second in this tumultuous world of ours, there exists a moment in time at which brand marketers have a unique opportunity to seize the popularity and ride the wave of a breaking story to benefit their brand in some fashion. The time span for such a story is typically hours or days. Most of us know all too well, the popularity of a news story often dies off quickly. But there are a few news opportunities that last weeks.

The impact of seizing a timely story early to benefit your business is big, especially compared to the effort you had to put out to get in on the mix. Newsjacking is fairly simple. The key is *thinking and acting fast.*

Here are some tips on how to develop effective Newsjacking strategies:

* Set yourself up to track major news outlets via RSS feeds and social media.
* Stay up on industry newsletters, emails and subscriptions. In business, news can develop slowly, but give yourself ample time to join in on the discussions.

- Check keyword search volumes for the topics that are most relevant to your brand, message, and products and services.
- Move as fast as possible. Newsjacking is primarily built on speed.
- Create quality content, but remember, speed is your primary concern.
- Work on getting the word out, pushing your content to those which will find it intriguing, timely and an important addition or angle to the story. This is where your social network, email lists, and contacts in the media come in handy.
- Make sure that your use of Newsjacking promotes the right type of message aligned with your brand identity and strategy.

Giving your audience what content they seek in a manner that is relevant, timely, and useful, is a successful long-term strategy that will establish and guarantee that your ***Power Brand*** is a part of the important and trending conversations and topics of its times.

CHAPTER 28

The Rousing Side of Power Branding

THE MAJORITY OF THIS BOOK is dedicated to the science, technologies, methods and techniques of power branding. But if we left it up to the mechanics exclusively, we would omit the very essence and the fun of successful *Power Brands*.

Power Brands believe in their purpose and mission completely. They arouse others to believe, to belong and to take action.

Branding is more than a mundane series of business processes, production, and consumption. Of course, businesses are meant to be profitable, but if this series is the be-all-end-all of business, starting and owning a new business would not be the right stuff of dreams for millions of entrepreneurs worldwide.

Brands are an integral part of our lives; they define us to others. Brands are sources of self-expression that embody our beliefs: how we fit, what our roles are inside of our cultures and our sub-cultures; even why we exist on Earth.

Harley-Davidson, Toms, Patagonia, Victoria's Secret – even the NRA (National Rifle Association) – are among the best-known brands

Create a video book trailer. A book trailer is a great way to define your book. Remember, people are more likely to watch a video than read. And YouTube is the second largest search engine in the world.

Video book trailers get the attention of your potential readers and spark their excitement. In many ways, a trailer can be an author's best brand content to engage and enthuse potential buyers to become loyal fans and followers. Video presents a golden marketing opportunity and a great way to generate buzz, because video can be shared on social media and is more engaging than written content alone.

The digital age has given writers, as well as readers, something not available before—an instant method of reaching and sharing with audiences and new fans. The dialogue between readers and writers used to be one-way. With social media and online content, readers can get to know their authors and engage in *genuine* two-way dialogues with them. (A word of caution, however: do not alienate your potential readers. Unless the driving force of your novel involves politics, stay clear of controversial issues, even when baited to discuss them.)

The internet has enough trolls and anti-social types to darken anyone's days; don't let a few negative individuals involve you in petty arguments and drag you down to their debased level.

Just remember, the internet is a public space and anyone can watch what you say and how you interact with others. Take the high ground: treat all comments (even negative ones) with common sense. You will discover that your loyal readers and ardent followers will be the best ones to defend you.

Give something away. Promotions always catch the interest of readers—especially when they see a product offered free or at a deeply discounted price. Online promotions via social media outlets are a great way to attract the attention of your readers and to keep your book sales up.

Building partnerships works as part of book promotions. Once you know your platform, reach out to organizations with *similar interests* or target audiences to yours. For instance, find bloggers with a comparable focus, who are willing to promote your book. Find companies willing to give your readers free products for using their services. When everyone works toward the same end, partnerships can be beneficial for everyone involved. You just have to know your platform inside and out before building a partnership; otherwise, you could partner with people or causes that are either unrelated or antithetical to your cause. In that case, you would be sending your readers mixed (confusing) messages, which will surely have a bad effect on your sales.

Hire a Literary Agent, if you can afford one and you are looking to get published by a "traditional" publishing house. However, with the advent of the eBook and on-demand printing, independent (self) publishing has definitely become more accessible and viable for a broad base of aspiring scribes.

When searching for a literary agent and you are not a celebrity, you will need to have a finished and polished *manuscript*, if you are submitting a novel or memoir. If you submit a nonfiction project, a finished and polished *proposal*, which includes three to five sample chapters from your book, will be required. Referrals are a great way to find an agent, and for many literary agents a great referral is not only essential, but a requirement.

This gives him months of a continuous stream of "fresh" content. Google and his audience notices his consistency of messaging and postings.

STEP 7: DISTRIBUTE THIS CONTENT OVER TIME.

As well as optimizing it for local search, the owner realizes that he will need to be much more proactive in distributing his content. So, he decides to email one video and one blog post per week. Again, this gives him practically a half-years' worth of email marketing content that keeps his email audience engaged. Over time, he witnesses that his emails are being shared, inspiring more word-of-mouth sharing, and those powerful share signals hit the eyes of Google. As he makes more money, he decides to pay for his videos to show up in a YouTube paid campaign. He does the same with Google and Facebook with landing pages, repurposing the content from his videos and blog posts.

STEP 8: SOCIAL CONTAGION.

To ensure that he has a continuous stream of social signals, the owner of Cafe 08 now leverages the power automated, social media management. With social management resources such as Hootsuite, Buffer, SocialOomph, SroutSocial or Klout, he knows that he can further re-purpose his blog content into individual social posts. One individual blog post can be cut up into dozens of tweets.

Photos of the event (and the coffee and food on hand) are posted daily on Instagram. He preloads all of this content for a week's worth of social shares, with links pointed back to his other content, and to all of his followers; this not only frees up his time, but also gets his content retweeted, liked and shared on a routine basis.

STEP 9: LEVERAGE THE POWER OF ONLINE REVIEWS.

The best content is user-generated content. Development of a proactive mindset and marketing strategy, which leverages the growing influence of online reviews, is key. While Yelp and Google My Business are the most effective for SEO purposes, there are many others worth paying attention to, which can gain more reviews.

Our owner at Cafe 08 realizes that he needs to leverage this opportunity and to engage with some type of automated software that will make this process easier and more effective. He discovers a reputation management company, such as Reputation Express (ReputationExpressPro.com), and utilizes their services to generate and distribute dozens upon dozens of positive online reviews.

STEP 10: REPURPOSE ALL THE CONTENT INTO AN EBOOK OR BOOK.

Here's how the owner now elevates himself to author status. The transcript from his videos, as well as his blogs and other materials can be repackaged into a book or eBook. More than likely, the owner has no time to write the book himself, so he hires a ghostwriter to do it for him. Within a few months, his book "For the Love of Coffee" is now published, gaining even more press and ardent followers. He is now regarded as a "coffee expert."

The result? Cafe 08 wins the marketing game Big Time!

THE SCALABILITY OF THIS METHOD

This SEO and content marketing strategy is completely scalable in several ways:

* Hold more events. Live and via webinars.
* Invite even more people to these events.

* Create more content per event.
* Create different angles of valuable and insightful content.
* Create a wider variety of content, such as infographics and podcasts.
* Leverage the help of additional professionals, such as event planners, writers, editors, SEO geeks, etc.

The only limit to this plan is your ingenuity, enthusiasm, ambition and resources. And here is my shameless plug: I offer a service, *Premier Expert,* which is a "done-for-you" marketing program that incorporates all these actions. You can find out more about it at PowerBrandingSecrets.com.

There you have it. What will you do with it now?

CHAPTER 32

Where to Begin

"The secret to getting ahead is getting started." — Mark Twain

So, HERE WE ARE AT the last chapter. I am sure by now you have already begun to craft a strategy and develop some branded content. You may even have become a bit more active in connecting with others on social media.

You are on your way to having a true ***Power Brand*** with ***Power Brand Strategies***!

Congratulations!

The reality is that there is not only much information provided by this book, but also resource listings and individual linkages, which can expand your work to almost infinite results. It would be so easy for you now to become overwhelmed by the sheer amount of resources available, so much that you end up doing nothing. Do not allow your fresh ideas and rough plans scribbled down to become abandoned on that yellow pad, or left floating about somewhere on the Google Doc cloud.

Not to worry. We have that covered, too.

THE POWER OF ONE

Start with one thing, one step, one channel or one type of branded content.

"Where do I begin?" is answered with, "Where do you feel the most comfortable beginning?"

I recall working with a chiropractor in Orange County, CA, who had a small office and a part-time office girl. That was the totality of his practice. He knew he needed to address his branding and marketing, but just the utterance of those words put him into a bit of a mental tail spin. This was the simple program that I laid out for him:

1. Find one artist to design a modern logo.
2. Send out one email per week to your list.
3. Curate at least one review on Yelp and Google per week from your existing patient base.
4. Continue to do 2 and 3 on a weekly basis.

Two things occurred as a result: first, he had begun to do something positive about growing his practice. Progress is progress. Secondly, he was growing his practice, because what little marketing that he did now was more than he had done before. The point is this: regardless of how little you have, something – some one thing – can be done right now. Something can be achieved.

"Start where you are. Use what you have. Do what you can." - Arthur Ashe

Arthur Ashe was astute in his observation. We begin where we already are. We leverage what we already have with more effectiveness. We do what we can do and then we become better, more confident.

In the case of this chiropractor, he had an email list, he had a business listing on Yelp and he had patients. That's where we began. As he grew, he had more financial resources to conduct additional marketing actions. Maybe he spent some money with a retired chiropractor who loved to write articles. Maybe he hired a local videography student to shoot some short "how to" videos on back and neck exercises.

Well, I think you get the point now.

Wherever you are, Start!

Whatever you have to hand, Act!

Whatever can you do, Do it!

Proof

42234974R00136

Made in the USA
Charleston, SC
19 May 2015